"So Hank
Says
to Yogi..."

"So Hank Says to Yogi . . ."

The Best
Baseball Stories
Ever Told

KEVIN NELSON

Chamberlain Bros.

a member of Penguin Group (USA) Inc.

New York

2005

CHAMBERLAIN BROS.
Published by the Penguin Group
Penguin Group (USA) Inc., 375 Hudson Street, New York, New York 10014, USA
Penguin Group (Canada), 10 Alcorn Avenue, Toronto, Ontario M4V 3B2, Canada
(a division of Pearson Penguin Canada Inc.)
Penguin Books Ltd, 80 Strand, London WC2R 0RL, England
Penguin Ireland, 25 St Stephen's Green, Dublin 2, Ireland
(a division of Penguin Books Ltd)
Penguin Group (Australia), 250 Camberwell Road, Camberwell, Victoria 3124,
Australia (a division of Pearson Australia Group Pty Ltd)
Penguin Books India Pvt Ltd, 11 Community Centre, Panchsheel Park,
New Delhi–110 017, India
Penguin Group (NZ), Cnr Airborne and Rosedale Roads, Albany, Auckland 1310,
New Zealand (a division of Pearson New Zealand Ltd)
Penguin Books (South Africa) (Pty) Ltd, 24 Sturdee Avenue, Rosebank,
Johannesburg 2196, South Africa
Penguin Books Ltd, Registered Offices: 80 Strand, London WC2R 0RL, England

An application has been submitted to register this book with the Library of Congress.
ISBN 1-59609-014-6

Printed in the United States of America

10 9 8 7 6 5 4 3 2 1

Book design by Jaime Putorti

Contents

Introduction

Some years ago, Don Wade wrote a book titled *And Then Jack Said to Arnie . . .* A collection of some of the best golf stories of all time, the book proved so popular that Don did a second collection, and a third, and a fourth, until (by unofficial count) there are now at least ten books in this ongoing series.

If, as the old saying goes, imitation is the sincerest form of flattery, then Don Wade should feel very flattered indeed, for his books are the inspiration for this one—a collection of more than 300 of the best stories baseball has to offer.

Baseball and golf have much in common. Each has a long, colorful history with plenty of colorful characters and stories. *"So Hank Says to Yogi . . ."* contains both the old and new, the past and present, from Babe Ruth and Walter Johnson, to Yogi Berra and Mickey Mantle, to Derek Jeter and Ichiro and other stars of today.

My profound gratitude to Don Wade. Thanks also to my agent, Gene Brissie, who happened to have lunch one day with Carlo DeVito, who had the idea for this book and was looking for a writer to do it. Gene suggested my name, and we were on our way. Thanks as well to Ron Martirano for his editorial support and guidance.

—Kevin Nelson

Sandy Alderson

When it comes to turbocharged résumés, it is hard to top Sandy Alderson's. A graduate of Dartmouth College and Harvard Law, an attorney and former officer with the United States Marines, Alderson is executive vice president of baseball operations for Major League Baseball. Before taking his current job, he served as general manager of the Oakland Athletics, another title for his résumé.

What made his stint with the Athletics so impressive is that Alderson helped build the championship Oakland teams of the late '80s, featuring such stars as Jose Canseco, Dennis Eckersley, Rickey Henderson, Mark McGwire, Dave Stewart, and manager Tony LaRussa. A bespectacled, intensely bright man—*Sports Illustrated* called him "the most respected mind in the game today"—who could nevertheless be Marine-tough when he needed to be, Alderson set a casual tone in the Oakland front office, occasionally wearing shorts and sandals while on the job, a sartorial habit also practiced by an Alderson protégé who now occupies Alderson's former post with the A's, Billy Beane.

Coming into the '88 World Series, the American League champion Athletics were heavy favorites to whip the Los Angeles Dodgers, champions of the National League. The Dodgers had a terrific pitcher (23-game-winning Orel Hershisher—the new owner of the consecutive scoreless innings streak), an injured slugger (National League Most Valuable Player Kirk Gibson, hobbling around with a torn hamstring and a sprained knee), and not much else to frighten the A's, who had won the AL West by 13 games and powdered Eastern Division champ Boston in four. With the muscle-bound Bash Brothers of McGwire and Canseco in their lineup, the A's appeared to be a reincarnation of the '27 Yankees.

In the first game of the Series at Dodger Stadium, the A's led 4 to 3 entering the bottom of the ninth. On the hill was their glamorous star reliever, Dennis Eckersley, with his stylish mustache and long brown hair jutting out from under the back of his green cap. But Eckersley, perhaps pitching too carefully to ex-teammate Mike Davis, who had come over to the Dodgers that year after eight seasons with the A's, walked him to put a man on first with two out and the ailing Gibson advancing to the plate.

It was speculated that because of his injuries, Gibson, a solidly built former Michigan State wide receiver who could barely walk, would not play at all in the Series. But knowing how important this moment was, not only in the game but in setting the tone for the Series, Dodgers manager Tommy Lasorda sent him up to pinch-hit.

Various fan polls have named what happened next as the greatest single event in Los Angeles sports history and one of the most memorable in all of sports history. The left-handed-hitting Gibson, who until then had spent much of the game in the training room receiving treatment for his leg, sent an Eckersley pitch into the right-field seats for a game-winning two-run home run. As the limping but exhilarated Gibson rounded the bases, pumping his fist, and his teammates rushed onto the field and a sold-out Dodger Stadium crowd turned to bedlam, Jack Buck's broadcast call seemed to capture the profound shock of the moment, the sheer hallucinogenic improbability of it all: "I don't believe what I just saw! I don't believe what I just saw!" No one else did either, including Sandy Alderson.

Throughout the next game, and the ones that followed, all the media could talk about was the story of the Gibson homer. How Lasorda, seeing Eckersley warming up in the bullpen for the ninth, had called for him in the training room. And then how Gibson had taken his warm-up cuts in the indoor batting cage at Dodger Stadium, wincing in pain with every swing, before emerging from the dugout for the only at bat he would take in the entire Series.

Listening to this story repeated seemingly endlessly, the most respected mind in the game was up to his ears in it. After the Series ended—inspired by the miracle of Game 1, the underdog Dodgers turned conventional wisdom on its head, besting the A's in five—Alderson ordered the construction of an indoor batting cage at the Oakland Coliseum, which previously did not have one. The cage exists to this day and A's hitters use it to practice their swings, just the way Gibson did that night at Dodger Stadium. It is called the Kirk Gibson Memorial Batting Cage.

Richie Ashburn

Some baseball teams were so distinctive that they became known by more than just their team name.

The Hitless Wonders. The Miracle Braves. The Black Sox. The Gas House Gang. The Daffiness Boys. The Amazin' Mets. The Big Red Machine.

The Whiz Kids were another of these storied teams. As any die-hard fan of Philly baseball can tell you, they were the 1950 Philadelphia Phillies, and they got their name because they were young and they were good. They featured 21-year-old lefty ace Curt Simmons, 24-year-old righty ace Robin Roberts, 25-year-old RBI man Del Ennis, and they came into the final game of that season needing only to beat the Dodgers at Ebbets Field in Brooklyn to claim Philadelphia's first National League pennant in 35 years.

Roberts, making his third start in only five days, went up against the best the Dodgers had, Don Newcombe, and the two men took a 1–1 tie into the bottom of the ninth. With the Philly right-hander tiring, Brooklyn outfielder Cal Abrams started the inning with a single and went to second on another single by Pee Wee Reese, bringing the dangerous Duke Snider to the plate. Snider cracked a hard single to center, sending Abrams around third and headed for home.

Fielding the ball cleanly in center was the whizziest of the Whiz Kids, 23-year-old Richie Ashburn, who, though not known for a strong arm, threw a strike to 25-year-old Phillies catcher Stan Lopata, who tagged Abrams out by a mile. This killed the Dodger rally and they failed to score. In the next inning, the top of the tenth, 26-year-old Dick Sisler knocked a three-run home run to claim the game and the flag for the Phillies, and at long last their fans had something to celebrate.

Though the Yankees swept them in four games in the World Series, the Whiz Kids retain to this day a prominent place in Philadelphia baseball lore, in part because of the vividness of the personalities on that team, most notably the man who made the throw to save the pennant, Richie Ashburn. Called "Whitey" affectionately by his teammates for his light complexion and hair, Ashburn was not lacking in color, not at all. He was, to borrow a phrase, his own self. There was nobody else like Whitey.

Robin Roberts found this out in 1948 when they both reported to the Phillies' spring training camp in Clearwater, Florida. Both were new to the bigs, and when the club moved up north to begin the regular season, they lived together in a boardinghouse run by Ashburn's parents. Being rookies and teammates, and talented ones at that, they quickly became friends. "We played cards, argued, shot pool, and argued some more," said Roberts, describing those days.

One of the things they argued about was driving. One time the two of them were going to a game and Roberts, who was behind the wheel, ran through what he thought was a yellow light. A traffic cop thought different and pulled them over. When Roberts started to make his case to the officer that the light was really yellow and he shouldn't be ticketed, the man riding with him disagreed.

"No, no, Officer," said Richie. "You're right. The light was red."

As fast as they come ("That kid has twin motors in his pants," Ted Williams said about him), Ashburn ran down every fly ball hit his way in center field, batted leadoff with a .333 average, stole a league-leading 32 bases, and won the 1948 Rookie of the Year honors.

He was just young enough and arrogant enough to think a pitcher should never get him out. *Ever.*

Those times when he struck out he'd walk back to the dugout still yelling at the man on the mound. "You ain't got nothin'," he'd say. "How'd you get me out with stuff like that?"

His teammates on the bench would just shake their heads and laugh. That was just Richie being Richie.

Off the field, he was just the same. A guy who loved to compete but who loved to win even more. "Tell your troubles to Jesus," he'd say to other Whiz Kids after taking their money in poker or gin rummy.

One of the guys he liked to compete against was his roomie, Robin Roberts, who was establishing a reputation as a pitcher every bit as good and perhaps even better than what Ashburn was doing in center field. In 1950, the year of the Whiz Kids, Roberts began a run of six straight seasons of 20 wins or more, with a high point of 28 wins and 7 losses in 1952. A control pitcher with pop on his fastball, the durable, hardworking Roberts was in the midst of what would become a Hall of Fame career.

Beating his pal, however, was another story.

In tennis, Richie let Robin hit to his side using the doubles lines, while Richie used only the singles lines against Robin. This gave Robin a big advantage, because the side of the court he could hit to was much wider. Even so, Richie usually whipped him.

Their Ping-Pong duels were even more lopsided. The first time they played, Richie whipped Robin 21 to 2. The next game he spotted him 15 points and won, 21 to 17. Their third game he played left-handed and still won, 21–19. After that, Robin declared that he was never playing Ping-Pong with Richie again.

Robin thought he was a better basketball player than Ashburn, though of course Richie would never admit to this. "If Richie was on your team and you wanted to work on your assists," Roberts once said, "he was happy to oblige. But he was not likely to pass a ball back. He thought a basketball was made to shoot, and that was what he did with it."

Pepper is a baseball warm-up game in which one player bats and one or more players field. The players in the field stand several paces away from the batter and make light tosses to him. The batter then taps the ball back to them in a lively manner and they play back and forth, practicing their hitting and fielding.

When Richie Ashburn played pepper, he'd try to hit the ball back against the other player's shins.

In Shibe Park in Philadelphia, where the Phillies of this era played, there was a mound near the home dugout that was used by pitchers to warm up before the start of a game. One day Robin Roberts was taking his practice pitches on this mound when Ashburn came and stood at the plate with a bat in his hands, as if he were about to hit. This was, and is, a routine occurrence in pregame warm-ups: A batter stands at the plate so that the pitcher is not just playing catch with the catcher, but has the sense of pitching to an actual hitter—though the man with the bat only watches the pitches go by and never swings.

Except in this case Roberts threw a pitch and Ashburn *swung* at it, chipping the ball over the dugout and into the seats, where it hit an unsuspecting fan in the face. The Phillies had to pay a financial settlement to this fan because of the accident.

Afterward, Robin asked his friend, "What were you thinking? What were you doing? Why'd you swing?"

"It looked so good," said Richie, "I had to rip at it."

One time Richie called Robin to see if he wanted to put some money into an apartment investment in Richie's native Nebraska. After hearing Richie describe it, Robin said it sounded like a great opportunity and agreed to go in on the deal.

Then, a few days later, Richie called Robin back to say that Robin couldn't participate after all. The deal was just too sweet, and Richie was going to put up all the money himself.

In his 12 seasons with the Phillies, Ashburn won two batting titles and finished second in batting three times. But eventually his performance fell off and Philadelphia traded him to the Cubs. After a couple of seasons in Chicago, he came over to the New York Mets in 1962, the same year his old buddy Robin Roberts left Philadelphia for another club. The former Whiz Kids were no longer kids and no longer teammates.

The Mets were then in the first year of their existence, a newly formed expansion team with a legendary manager in Casey Stengel and, except for the 35-year-old Ashburn and power-hitting Frank Thomas in left field, not much in the way of ballplaying talent. But Casey knew all about Ashburn—in Casey's typically mangled phrase-making style, he referred to his former club as "the Quiz Kids"—and put him in center field, where Richie quickly developed problems with Mets shortstop Elio Chacon.

On short fly balls to center, Ashburn would yell, "I got it! I got it!"—calling off the other fielders so he could make the putout. But the energetic Chacon, a Venezuelan native who spoke no English, would ignore what his center fielder was saying, run out from the infield, and smash into Ashburn if Richie didn't get out of his way and let him catch the ball.

Frustrated by this, Ashburn approached a bilingual teammate, who advised him to call off Chacon in Spanish: *"Yo la tengo."*

This sounded like the perfect solution, but Richie first wanted to clear it with Chacon. Approaching him at his locker before a game, he said, " *'Yo la tengo'?"*

"Sí," said Chacon enthusiastically. *"¡Yo la tengo!"*

Having arrived at an understanding, Ashburn took the field that day with Chacon at short. The inevitable shallow pop fly to center came, with Richie yelling as loud as he could, *"¡Yo la tengo! ¡Yo la tengo!"*

Hearing these words, Chacon immediately backed off, and as Richie was set to make the catch, Frank Thomas barreled into him and knocked him to the ground.

Ashburn finished that year with a .306 average, the ninth time in his career he had hit .300 or above for a season. The Mets declared him their Most Valuable Player and gave him a boat.

That was his last year as a player. His old club, the Phillies, was looking around for someone to add some color to their radio broadcasts. If anybody could add color to a broadcast, it was Whitey Ashburn. He joined the Phillies' broadcast team and, partnered with Harry Kalas, stayed there for the next 35 years or so. Elected to the Hall of Fame in 1995, Ashburn died two years later at age 70.

In 2004, the Phillies opened their new ballpark, Citizens Bank Park. Among its features were four ten-foot-high bronze statues of four Philadelphia Hall of Famers: Steve Carlton, Mike Schmidt, and the two former Whiz Kids, Robin Roberts and Richie Ashburn.

Emmett Ashford

Emmett Ashford as a teenager achieved a number of firsts, among them first black student body president of Jefferson High School in Los Angeles, and first black editor of the school's paper. But Emmett loved baseball too, and one day at a semipro game when the umpire did not appear as scheduled, he volunteered to stand in for him.

Some of the white players and fans objected to this. In the 1930s, blacks could (and did) play with whites in school and semipro ball, but who had ever heard of a black umpire? The umpire is in charge; what he says, goes. Players and managers must accept his decisions or be tossed from the game. Having Ashford as the umpire meant that the whites on the field had to respect whatever he said and defer to him.

The teenager insisted he could do the job, and the two teams agreed to give him a try. The game went on, and Ashford made his debut as an umpire. He even got paid a little something for his work.

When Jackie Robinson joined the Brooklyn Dodgers in 1947, breaking the color barrier in major league baseball, it led to other breakthroughs by other blacks in other realms of the game. One of these breakthroughs occurred in the early 1950s when Emmett Ashford became the first black umpire in organized baseball. Having umped high school and college games for many years in southern California, and then left his steady job as a postal worker for a season in Mexican professional baseball, he joined the Class C Southwest International League in El Paso.

Predictably, some of the antagonism he encountered had to do not with his calling of balls and strikes but with the color of his skin.

"Why don't you go back to where you came from?" one fan yelled from the stands. "I don't want you doing a white man's job."

Emmett turned and coolly said to him, "If you go home and put on some shoes, then we can discuss the matter."

With his reputation growing as a man who could withstand the heckling of fans (and, upon occasion, give it back to them), Ashford umpired a 1953 exhibition game between the Yomiuri Giants and the New York Giants in Santa Maria, California. This was the first time a pro team from Japan had traveled to the United States after World War II.

The following year, Emmett joined the Pacific Coast League, where he served for 12 seasons (the last two as a crew chief) and firmly established his reputation as a man with his own unique style. Years ahead of his time in men's fashion, he appreciated fine clothes and dressed well, sporting rings and jewelry and cuff links that sparkled. On the field, when not umpiring behind the plate, Emmett sprinted out to his position at first or third base. Short and stocky, he got his whole body into it when he made an out call, which made him popular with fans but not so popular with players and managers.

One Coast League manager always called him "Vomit." While arguing a call with him once, this manager said, "You missed that one, Vomit. You make me Emmett."

In 1966, Ashford joined the American League, achieving another first: the first black umpire in the major leagues. He umpired there for four years.

George Bamberger

If anyone paid his dues in the minor leagues, it was George Bamberger. He pitched more than 20 years in the minors, appearing only briefly with the Giants and Orioles in the majors. But the Staten Island–born right-hander spent all that time in the bushes wisely, learning how to teach his craft even if he could not do it at the highest level. After retiring from active play, he joined the Orioles' farm system as an instructor, and in 1968 he joined the big league club as its pitching coach under Earl Weaver.

Bamberger was the perfect man to advise Weaver, who was then in his first year managing the team and whose recipe for baseball success was admirably simple: "Pitching, defense, and the three-run homer." Bamberger's philosophy as pitching coach was equally without frills. "What you have to do is B.S.," he said when asked how to succeed as a pitching coach. "That is the only way you can get maximum ability out of each individual."

Whatever he did, it worked. In his nine seasons with the O's, he produced a flock of 20-game winners and Cy Young Award recipients. In 1971, four Orioles pitchers—Mike Cuellar, Chuck Dobson, Dave McNally, and Jim Palmer—won 20 or more games apiece, only the second time in baseball history that four pitchers from the same team have each won 20 or more games in a season.

With all his success in Baltimore, Bamberger became the leading candidate to take over the hapless Milwaukee Brewers, which had won only 67 games in 1977, finishing in sixth place in the American League East.

Bud Selig, the current Commissioner of Baseball, who was then president of the Brewers, met Bamberger for the first time at the University Club in Milwaukee while recruiting him to take over the team. Selig could see, as he said later, that Bamberger was "perfect for Milwaukee": a balding, somewhat portly man in his early fifties with a fondness for the drink that made Milwaukee famous. He loved beer and drank it regularly, a trait that endeared him to the city's baseball fans. Fans also liked the fact that Bamberger was a blunt-spoken man who said what was on his mind, something Selig discovered about him at their first meeting.

"I hope you're coming to Milwaukee," said Selig, who wanted to hire Bamberger though George had not yet made up his mind to take the job.

"You know," he responded, "you guys are a bunch of losers."

Even so, Bamberger took the job and the next season guided the Brewers to their first winning season in franchise history, capturing 93 games and finishing third in their division.

The Brewers of that era featured a host of budding young stars— including rookies Paul Molitor and Robin Yount, both of whom are now in the Hall of Fame—and came to be known as Bambi's Bombers in honor of their skipper, who would, after home games, mingle with fans at Ray Jackson's restaurant on West Blue Mound Road in Milwaukee, eating ham sandwiches and drinking his fa- vorite beverage. Fans described him as the grandfather they all wished they had, though Bamberger had a temper too, frequently being thrown out of games for furiously arguing calls.

One of Bamberger's favorite players on that club was Gorman Thomas. Sporting long unkempt hair, a Fu Manchu mustache, and perpetually scruffy three-day-old whiskers, Gorman had the kind of face that, as one sportswriter said, "if he came into your home with your daughter, you'd disown them both." But Bamberger liked what he saw in the slugger whose reputation for home-run power was surpassed only by his unfortunate tendency to strike out.

On Opening Day 1978, Bamberger's first as a big-league manager, Thomas whiffed four times against the Orioles. But after the game, the manager sought him out and said, "Hey, you big son of a gun. I didn't need you today. Maybe you'll give me something tomorrow."

The next day, Thomas hit a grand slam.

Under Bamberger's grandfatherly tutelage, Thomas blossomed in center field for the Brewers. Fans dubbed him "Stormin' Gorman" for the all-out abandon with which he played. "The fans come to see me strike out, hit a home run, or run into a fence," he said. "I try to accommodate them at least one way every game."

Late in the '78 season, Stormin' Gorman got knocked unconscious after running into the outfield wall while chasing a fly ball. His skipper came running out of the dugout to see if he was all right.

"Did I catch it?" Thomas asked.

Never mind that, Bamberger told him. What he desperately wanted to know was: "Are you all right?"

But what Thomas wanted to know was whether or not he had caught the ball. And he wouldn't answer Bamberger's question until Bamberger answered his. Finally, his manager gave up.

"Yeah, you caught it," Bamberger grunted. "But the next time you do this, get off the ground so I don't have to run all the way out here to see if you're okay."

Thomas got off the ground to hit 32 home runs that season, his most ever in the majors by far, and the next year he topped that total with 45 to lead the American League. He also led the league in strikeouts that season, but that was just Stormin' Gorman being himself, giving the fans what they wanted to see.

After the Brewers won 95 games and took second place in 1979 to improve upon their finish the previous season, fans were looking forward to the 1980 season when they got the shocking news that

George Bamberger had had a heart attack in spring training in Arizona. He survived, but had to undergo bypass surgery that would prevent him from starting the season with the club.

After the surgery was over and Bamberger was recovering, a reporter asked his physician how George was doing now that he had to go on a diet that prevented him from drinking beer, at least for a while. "George and I have been negotiating in terms of how much beer he will be able to drink," the physician replied. "And I assure you, he's a tough negotiator."

Not long after that, on Opening Day, George delivered a taped message to Brewers fans on the County Stadium scoreboard: "I hope you all have a beer on me on Opening Day." Bamberger returned later in the season to run the club, only to decide that the travel and pressure of being a big league manager were too demanding. A year later, though, he was back in baseball with the New York Mets. He later came back to the Brewers for a second stint as their manager.

Yogi Berra

"He's one of those Christmas Eve guys. There are people like that. Every day in their lives is Christmas Eve."

—Joe Garagiola, on Yogi Berra

Southwest St. Louis had a neighborhood in the 1930s known as "The Hill." Mainly poor and working-class families of Italian descent lived there. The men on The Hill worked long hours in manual-labor jobs, and the women stayed home taking care of their children, who played games on the streets, often in their bare feet. One of the games they played—the favorite game of the boys—was baseball, and they would play all day long until the brickyard factory whistle rang and the boys raced over to Fassi's Tavern, grabbed containers of beer, and hustled them home. No boy wanted to risk having his father come home and not have his pitcher of beer waiting for him at the end of a hard workday.

One of the boys who delivered beer for his father and whose parents came from the old country was Joe Garagiola, who grew up to be a major league ballplayer and a famous television broadcaster. The Garagiolas lived on Elizabeth Avenue on The Hill. Across the street from them were the Berras: Pietro, who, like Giovanni Garagiola, was a bricklayer and a native of Italy; his wife Paulina, also a native of Italy; and their five children, Josie, John, Mike, Tony, and another boy, Lawrence—known today and for all time as Yogi.

Like his buddy Joe, Lawrence Berra (he wasn't Yogi yet) made sure he delivered beer on time to his papa in the late afternoon before dinner. Also like Joe, he attended mass at St. Ambrose Church with his family every Sunday. Neither Yogi nor Joe played Little League; there weren't any organized leagues on The Hill. They just played and played and played. Sometimes they played kids from the nearby Irish and German neighborhoods, their games taking place on an empty lot that doubled as a garbage dump. On this lot were two junk cars. But Yogi and Joe and the other kids didn't think of them as junk. They pretended they were major league dugouts.

Both Yogi and Joe got pretty good at baseball—sometimes when they were on the same team Yogi pitched and Joe caught, and sometimes the reverse—and after a while major league scouts started to show up on The Hill to watch them play. Considered a better prospect at the time, Joe received a $500 bonus to sign with the hometown Cardinals, who also offered a contract to Yogi, but for less money. Yogi wouldn't take it, saying he deserved as much as his friend. But the Cardinals lost interest in him at the higher price.

The Cardinals' failure to sign Yogi provided an opening for the New York Yankees, who decided to pay the youngster what he wanted. It proved a wise move. Yogi went on to become one of the game's all-time great catchers, winning three Most Valuable Player Awards and playing on ten world championship teams in New York.

Berra's rookie season was 1947, the year of a Subway Series between his Yankees and the Dodgers of Brooklyn (the first of several to come). If baseball fans need any proof that the game has indeed changed and we are living in different times, this is it: To get to the games at Yankee Stadium and Ebbets Field, Yogi rode the subway.

Despite the honors that would later come his way, and the universal affection in which he would be held, Yogi had a rough time of it when he broke in with the Yankees. People made fun of how he looked. Mickey Mantle, who would later join him in New York and become his friend, described him as not "the handsomest man in the world . . . a short, stocky man with a powerful build and a short neck, a fairly homely face, a deep guttural voice, and a way of speaking that didn't sound much like Harvard."

Others were much less kind. Yankees president Larry MacPhail joked that Yogi "looked like the bottom man on an unemployed acrobatic team." Sportswriters said he looked better with his catcher's mask on. Some of his opponents said he resembled a monkey, calling him "The Ape" and mocking him by making ape sounds and gestures from their dugout. The heckling hurt Yogi deeply, though he outwardly brushed it off.

"So I'm ugly?" he said. "So what? I never saw anyone hit with his face."

★   ★   ★

The people back home, the people who watched him grow up on The Hill, stuck by Yogi and supported him always. When the Yankees traveled to Sportsman's Park in St. Louis to play the Browns in his rookie year, all the people from the old neighborhood came out to see him receive an award. Nervous about speaking in public, Yogi asked his bright, well-spoken roommate, third baseman Bobby Brown, to write a speech for him.

"I want to thank everyone who made this night possible," wrote Brown, and Yogi practiced the speech maybe a hundred times beforehand. But when it came time to deliver the words in front of all those fans in his hometown park, a park he used to come to as a boy, Yogi said instead, "I want to thank everyone who made this night necessary," botching the line, but saying something that turned out to be far more memorable and lasting.

People heckled the young Yogi for his looks, but more serious for him, at least in terms of his future in the game, some baseball experts criticized him for his playing abilities. He could always hit, but he appeared clumsy and lacked polish and adequate skills as a catcher. Bucky Harris, his manager in 1947 and 1948, even tried him in the outfield, which prompted another of Yogi's more famous lines: "It gets late early out there," his assessment of the harsh sun he encountered in left field at Yankee Stadium.

By the spring of 1949, though, a new Yankees manager had arrived on the scene. He was Casey Stengel. The old man liked Berra, saw the potential in him despite his struggles, and hired Bill Dickey to teach Yogi the fine art of catching. Dickey, an all-time-great Yankees catcher himself, who had retired from the game a few years earlier, showed the 23-year-old Berra how to squat down into a proper catcher's crouch, how to come up firing when a runner tries to steal a base, how to frame a close pitch with your glove so that the umpire will call it a strike, what pitches to call in various situations, and much more.

"Take pride in your position," Dickey told him. "It's the best job in baseball."

Yogi learned his lessons well, and when reporters asked him how he was doing that spring under Dickey's tutelage, he said, "Bill is learning me all his experiences," one more memorable line of Yogi's that, unlike so many others credited to him, he appears to have actually said.

With Bill Dickey as his mentor and Casey Stengel as his manager, Yogi's game behind the plate rose to match his proven ability to beat the stuffing out of the ball. He was, in baseball parlance, a bad-ball hitter, which meant that he swung at pitches outside of the strike zone that likely would have been called balls if he had just let them pass without offering at them. Left-hander Hal Newhouser of the Detroit Tigers grudgingly agreed that, yeah, Berra was a bad-ball hitter: "But I defy anybody to throw him a *good* ball." Yogi hit everything his bat could reach.

With a bat in his hands, Yogi was extremely eloquent; off the field, he was somewhat less so. One evening at a winter banquet, Joe Garagiola, who loved to talk as much as his friend did not, was presenting an award to Yogi. After Joe's long, rambling, funny introduction, Yogi finally stepped up to the dais to receive his award.

"Thanks," he said, sitting down and not uttering another word.

But nobody apparently minded, because people liked Yogi; he was a genuinely likable person. Together with his looks, and the funny things that occasionally came out of his mouth, it inspired others, mainly sportswriters and public relations people, to start making up things that Yogi supposedly said, and these Berraisms, as they are known, have become a staple of American life and a source of his widespread appeal.

One of the many people who loved to tell Yogi stories was the garrulous Garagiola, who talked about how a Yankees employee once called Yogi early in the morning to remind him of an appointment he had later in the day. When Yogi answered the phone, he sounded half asleep, and the employee apologized for waking him up.

"I'm sorry, Yogi," he said. "Did I get you out of bed?"

"Nah," said Yogi. "I had to get up to answer the phone anyway."

Yogi loved to read comic books. He read them all the time—on train trips when the Yankees were on the road, or in his hotel room relaxing before a game.

One day he and Bobby Brown were both reading quietly in their room. Being a premed student who was taking classes in the off-season to become a physician (a goal he ultimately realized), Brown intently absorbed a medical handbook, *Gray's Anatomy*. Meanwhile, Yogi was flipping through a Superman or some other comic.

When they both finished reading and put their books down, Yogi asked Bobby, "How did yours come out?"

His teammates liked to razz him for his comic book obsession, but Yogi had a ready response for them: "Yeah, right. I read comic books. But I notice that whenever I put them down, there are always some guys ready to pick them up."

When Yogi was a kid, a couple of his pals from The Hill went to a movie that had an Indian mystic, or yogi, in it. The yogi sat in a meditative position on the floor with his arms folded and legs crossed, much the way Yogi sometimes sat. So his friends started calling him by this name and it stuck.

Nevertheless, he still thought of himself as Lawrence, not Yogi, well after he had joined the Yankees. That is, until Bill McGowan, nearing the end of a distinguished four-decade umpiring career, asked him to autograph some balls for him, which Yogi did.

But McGowan took one look at the balls and was aghast. "Who the hell put Larry Berra on here?" he asked.

"I did," said Yogi. "It's my name."

"The hell it is," said McGowan, dismissing Yogi as if he had just called him out on strikes. "Sign them 'Yogi.' That's your name, ain't it?"

After that it certainly was. From that point on, all of Yogi's autographs were signed "Yogi," the way people wanted.

Despite his well-known distaste for speaking in public, Yogi was a chatterbox behind the plate. Casey Stengel said he acted "like home plate was his living room," talking to everybody he encountered—umpires, batboys, opposing hitters. It will come as no surprise that many hitters did not appreciate Yogi's ceaseless banter, the intent of which was, in part, to make them lose their concentration.

Some hitters told him to shut up. Others ignored him. Still others answered back.

It was during either the 1957 or 1958 World Series between the Braves and Yankees ('57 won by the Braves, '58 by the Yanks) that the menacing Hank Aaron advanced to the plate and Yogi told him that the label on his bat was pointing the wrong way.

"Yogi," said Hank, "I didn't come up here to read. I came up here to hit."

One day, Frank Scott, the former traveling secretary of the Yankees, was paying a visit to Yogi's house when he noticed some wristwatches lying on a table. He asked what they were for, and Yogi said he had received them as gifts for speaking engagements he had done. Surprised, Scott said that Yogi should be getting more, much more, when he made personal appearances or spoke in front of a group. Eventually, Scott started representing Yogi, becoming one of the earliest player agents in sports and arranging many of his off-season appearances, including guest spots on *The Ed Sullivan Show* and other TV programs of the era.

One of the product endorsements lined up for Yogi by Frank Scott was a cat food commercial. Yogi, appearing on camera, spoke to a cat, whose lips appeared to move but whose voice belonged to Yankee teammate Whitey Ford. Other Yankees, though not Ford, kidded Yogi about doing the commercial, but Yogi couldn't see what was wrong with it.

"So I asked them what was so funny? How many of them ever got nicely paid talking to a cat?"

Yogi and Phil Rizzuto, a Yankee teammate who later became a broadcaster for the club, jointly owned a bowling alley in New Jersey, Rizzuto-Berra Bowling Lanes. Yogi also became vice president of the Yoo Hoo Chocolate Drink Company. With these and other investments, plus his fees for his many product endorsements and speaking gigs, Yogi started doing pretty well for himself, a fact noticed by his manager.

"They say he's funny," Casey Stengel said. "Well, he has a lovely wife and family, a beautiful home, money in the bank, and he plays golf with millionaires. What's funny about that?"

Phil Rizzuto figures in another Yogi story (there are a million of them) in which Phil is driving to a banquet one evening with him. But Phil realizes they've lost their way.

"We're lost," he tells Yogi.

"Yeah," responds Yogi, "but we're making good time."

One time Yogi was sitting at home watching TV when he heard somebody—maybe old friend Joe Garagiola—tell how he had come out of a store and bumped into a friend who was carrying a grandfather clock.

"Geez," Yogi said, "why don't you wear a wristwatch like everyone else?"

After hearing this story (which was made up), Yogi commented, "If I could write lines like that, I'd be working for Bob Hope."

★   ★   ★

After Yogi's playing career with the Yankees ended, he managed the club to the pennant in 1964. Then he got fired, hiring on as a coach and very occasional catcher for the Mets the next season. On this same Mets club was 44-year-old Warren Spahn, taking the final few starts of his Hall of Fame pitching career, and he and the 40-year-old Berra may have formed the world's oldest battery, although Spahn wasn't sure about that.

"I don't know if we're the oldest," said Spahn, "but we sure are the ugliest."

Yogi loves the movies as much as he once loved comic books, and one Yogi story has his wife, Carmen, returning from the theater after seeing the 1965 David Lean classic *Doctor Zhivago*. "What," says Yogi, "are you sick or something?"

But Carmen enjoyed the film so much that Yogi apparently had to see it for himself, subsequently offering this capsule review: "Gee, it sure was cold in Russia in those days."

While working as a batting instructor for the Mets in the late '60s, Yogi tutored, among others, outfielder Ron Swoboda, who approached him for advice one day. Swoboda had enormous strength—"He could grind the dust out of the bat," said his former manager, Casey Stengel—but could not handle outside pitches. He felt that if he stood closer to the plate he could handle these pitches more successfully.

Yogi disagreed, saying that pitchers could then jam him easier with inside fastballs and he would not be able to fully extend his arms and get his bat-grinding power into his swing.

"But Frank Robinson does it that way," Swoboda complained, "and they don't jam him."

Frank Robinson was one of the best hitters of his time, a man who would end up with 586 career home runs and a berth in the Hall of Fame. Ron Swoboda was no Frank Robinson, but Yogi was too tactful—too smart—to insult one of his players in this manner. What he said was one of the wisest things he's ever uttered:

"That's because he's Frank Robinson and you're you," he told Swoboda. "That's his style of hitting. If you can't imitate him, don't copy him."

During the 1980s, Yogi and Carmen attended a State Dinner at the White House hosted by President Reagan. Another guest was Saudi Arabia's King Fahd, who spent much of the dinner conversing with Reagan. "The President chatted with the King a lot," said Yogi afterward. "I guess they've got a pretty good business going."

At one point in the dinner, though, Yogi got a chance to sit with King Fahd, though they didn't have much to say to each other. "All we did was exchange autographs," he recalled.

Later that same decade, a Little League team from Toms River, New Jersey, won the Little League World Series. As part of their victory celebration, the Toms River players and coaches came to New York as honored guests of the city, which included a meeting with Yogi. The parents of the Little Leaguers were excited about this prospect, but the players had never heard of him.

"We're going to see Yogi Bear?" one asked.

Yogi, who once said about Little League, "I think it's wonderful. It keeps the kids out of the house," thought this remark was hilarious and relayed the story himself.

Barry Bonds

The Bonds family of Riverside, California, was a particularly athletic one. One of the Bonds children, Robert, grew up to play professional football. Another of the Bonds kids, Rosie, participated in the 1964 Olympic Games as a hurdler for Team USA. Yet another talented Bonds offspring, Bobby, became a star outfielder for the San Francisco Giants. He was the first 30-30 man in baseball history: 30 home runs, 30 stolen bases in a single season.

A family man himself, Bobby Bonds had children of his own, including young Barry, who frequently visited the Giants' locker room in the late 1960s and early '70s when his father played for the team. As a kid, Barry got to practice with the grown-ups, throwing the ball around with his dad and his dad's teammates and swinging the heavy bats they used. Naturally, the youngster also saw lots of Giants games, sometimes collecting free bats as part of the Bat Day promotions held by the team.

Being a little guy and seeing how heavy these long pieces of sculpted wood were, Barry started to choke up on the handle of the bat when he batted—a habit he has carried into adulthood now that he is swinging a 34-inch, 31½-ounce stick of maple. "The free bats we got were heavy," explained Bonds. "I had to choke up. It became a habit."

Barry choked up on his bat when he starred in high school ball and for Arizona State University, and he was choking up the day in 1986 when Pirates general manager Syd Thrift came around to watch the 22-year-old left-hander hit batting practice. Thrift, a sharp-minded baseball man with a soft southern drawl, had taken the Pittsburgh job the previous fall despite the club's being in awful shape. Tarnished by drug scandals, in ailing financial health, the Pirates had finished in last place in 1985, losing 104 games. When asked how long it would take to revive the team, Thrift replied, "It ain't easy resurrecting the dead."

But there were signs of life. In November, after a meeting at the Green Tree Holiday Inn in Pittsburgh, Thrift hired Jim Leyland to run the club on the field. Though Leyland, then the third-base coach for the White Sox, had never managed in the big leagues before, his energy and intelligence won Thrift over and he signed him to a one-year contract.

Both Thrift and Leyland knew, though, that if they were really going to turn the Pirates around, they would need players, good players, which was what brought Thrift to the batting cage that day. The much-heralded Bonds, an All-American at Arizona State, had begun the 1986 season in the minors, and the Pittsburgh GM wanted to see if he was ready for the big time.

Bing. Bonds swung and the ball flew over the right-field fence. Bing. He swung again and another ball sailed over the right-field fence. Bing, bing, bing! Three more swings and three more balls over the fence.

Expressing his admiration, Thrift asked Barry to hit some balls the other way.

So then Bonds hit the next few pitches he saw over the *left field* fence. "How's that?" he said to Thrift, who, it is said, immediately ordered Bonds's call-up to Pittsburgh. There was no looking back for Bonds, as he never spent another day in the minor leagues.

With Jim Leyland developing into one of the best managers in the game, and the likes of Bonds, hard-hitting Bobby Bonilla, and defensive ace Andy Van Slyke in the outfield, the Pirates captured three straight National League East titles in the early 1990s. But Pittsburgh's title run ended in 1993, not coincidentally the same year

Bonds left the Pirates to sign with the team for which he had once served as a batboy and collected oversized bats.

In Bonds's first game as a San Francisco Giant, in his first time up in his first game at Candlestick Park, he hit a home run. As the ball soared over the right-field fence, he trotted down the first-base line and gave a high five to the first-base coach, who had been hired by the Giants after Barry signed with the team. It was his father, Bobby Bonds.

The precise moment when Bobby Bonds's son became recognized as the best player of his generation is not clear, but one contender among many choices was at a Candlestick night game on May 28, 1998, between the Giants and the visiting Diamondbacks. With the D-Backs leading 8 to 6 and two out in the bottom of the ninth, the home club had loaded the bases with Barry Bonds coming up to bat.

But Buck Showalter, the somber-faced Diamondbacks manager, had a different idea, a very different idea. He decided to have his pitcher intentionally walk Bonds rather than take the risk of pitching to him with the tying and winning runs on base.

Four wide pitches later, Bonds shed his black elbow protector and trotted to first base, forcing in a run and making the score 8 to 7, Diamondbacks. But next up for the Giants was Bret Mayne, a lefty-swinging catcher whose father was not Barry Bonds, whose godfather was not Willie Mays, who had never achieved All-American status at Arizona State, and who had never impressed anybody by hitting a half-dozen or so consecutive batting-practice pitches over the fence.

Buck Showalter liked the looks of this match-up much better—his pitcher, journeyman right-hander Gregg Olson, against Mayne—and it worked. Mayne hit a shot to right that found the soft padding of an outfielder's glove, ending the rally and the game with the Diamondbacks posting the W.

In the locker room afterward, Mayne was steaming: "They got

lucky. Bucky got lucky and Olson got lucky. If they do it again the next time, I'll hit another rocket. I've never seen it. In Little League, maybe, to a guy hitting .800. I hope he does it again. I thoroughly enjoyed that situation."

Perhaps. But results are what counts in baseball, and Showalter would not be the last manager to give a free pass to No. 25 in order to take his chances with the next hitter in the Giants' lineup.

Three years later, when Barry Bonds hit his 500th career home run—off Dodger pitcher Terry Adams, for those keeping track—his old boss, Syd Thrift, called Bonds to congratulate him. But as any sportswriter who has interviewed him will tell you, Bonds does not always give the answers that people expect.

"Most people would say, 'Thank you very much,'" recalled Thrift. "He told me, 'If you had brought me up to the majors earlier, I'd have hit it sooner.'" Thrift added with a laugh, referring to Bonds's young age when he came up from the minors, "If I had brought him up sooner, he would have been in an incubator."

For many years, the rap against Bonds was that he could not deliver in the postseason, having hit poorly in the playoffs and never making it to the World Series. But after the Giants won the 2002 National League pennant, he finally got his chance. With the Series opening in Anaheim against the Angels, winners of the American League pennant, Bonds walked up to the plate to face left-handed starter Jarrod Washburn in the first inning of the first game.

It was Bonds's first-ever at bat in Series competition, and Washburn ran two fastballs by him that were out of the strike zone. Then came another high fastball, foul-tipped by Bonds. The next ball, another hard one, was slightly inside and about belt high—"That's my favorite spot, right there," Bonds said later—and the man with a "swing as swift as a snake's bite," as one writer colorfully put it, jacked the pitch over the fence in right, into a tunnel used by maintenance workers.

A home run in his first World Series AB should have put to rest, permanently, any doubts about his ability to perform in the postseason, but, as if to make the point utterly clear to all, even perhaps including himself, Bonds hit another gigantic home run off Angels closer Troy Percival in Game 2 that made the millions of people watching on TV at home, the capacity crowd at Edison Field, and players on both teams shake their heads with the wonder of it all. "That's the farthest ball I've ever seen hit," said powerhouse Angels outfielder Tim Salmon, who has hit some pretty long, long balls himself in his career.

For the record, though the Giants lost the Series in seven, it would be hard to blame their failure on Bonds, who hit four home runs and achieved a gaudy slugging percentage despite being walked 13 times, seven intentionally, and being pitched to oh so very carefully each time he stepped into the batter's box.

Bobby Valentine, who managed against Bonds when Bobby was with the Mets, was talking about the Giants slugger and the persistent rumors of steroid use that have nagged him in recent years.

Like other baseball observers, the outspoken Valentine, who is now managing in Japan, has seen how the 6-foot-2-inch Bonds has grown from being a skinny 185-pounder into a heavy-packing 230-pounder with the body of a pro football linebacker. Bonds attributes his growth in size to a demanding year-round weight-lifting regime, but after his former trainer was indicted in the BALCO scandal for distributing steroids, Bonds's critics have said that a man his age could not have gained such muscle mass without chemical enhancements. In sealed grand jury testimony, Bonds admitted to unknowingly using substances made of synthetic steroids during the 2003 season.

But Valentine wasn't talking about any of that, exactly. What he was talking about was Bonds's extraordinary vision at the plate, how he can lay off balls a whisker or two outside the strike zone and then hit the stuffing out of pitches more suited to his liking. "Did they," asked Bobby, "shoot steroids in his *eyes*?"

One of the most memorable home runs of Bonds's career was No. 660, which tied the career total of Willie Mays, a onetime teammate of Barry's father. As a player, Mays combined speed and power in ways never before seen on a baseball field, and when Bobby Bonds, who was also gifted with speed and power, arrived on the scene, people said he was destined to become "the next Willie Mays." Though Bobby never quite fulfilled these lofty expectations (who could?), he became good friends with Willie, who acted as godfather to Bobby's little son, who was always poking around the Giants' locker room back then.

Over the years, Willie and the Bonds family remained close. When Barry, all grown up, joined the Giants in 1993, and especially after Bobby Bonds died of cancer ten years later, Willie served as Barry's mentor, friend, counselor, and coach in addition to godfather.

This was why reaching 660 was so memorable for Mays's godson. "He will always be the one I look up to," Bonds said of Willie. "He will always be the best baseball player of all time. That isn't ever going to change."

As for Mays, he is now in his seventies and serves as a special assistant to the Giants. His place in baseball history secure, a monumental statue of him stands outside SBC Park in San Francisco. After Bonds tied, and then, the next day, surpassed his lifetime home-run total, Mays recalled how, when Barry was a small child, his father had asked Willie to take care of his son if anything should happen to him.

"I think Bobby knew what he had in his son," said Willie. "Something special."

Frenchy Bordagaray

If you called Stanley Bordagaray by his first name, he may not have answered to it. For everyone in baseball knew him as "Frenchy," apparently a reference to his French Basque family roots. "The Bouncing Basque," sportswriters dubbed him.

Frenchy, who played 11 seasons in the majors, was as colorful as they come. In the early 1930s, while playing for the Sacramento Senators of the Pacific Coast League, he agreed to participate in a race against a horse. But at the last minute, the promoters of the event switched horses on him without his knowledge, exchanging the old plow horse Frenchy had agreed to race with a thoroughbred. Though fast, Frenchy was not that fast, and the thoroughbred whipped him easily.

Despite his liabilities as a ballplayer (great with a bat, not so good with a glove), the pint-sized Bordagaray thought a lot of himself. This was part of his charm: his cockiness. His first big league club was the Chicago White Sox, managed by Lew Fonseca. On the first day of spring training, a reporter asked Frenchy if he was going to play that day.

"Sure," he said breezily, "Fonseca is using all his regulars today."

Frenchy was never a regular for the Sox, played only 29 games for them that season, and got sent back down to the bushes. In August, in a game against Portland, Frenchy was in left field for Sacramento. But he didn't show for the ninth inning. His manager and teammates did not notice his absence, nor did the umpires. The batter at the plate did, though, taking advantage of the empty space by hitting a lazy fly into left for a stand-up double.

At that point, Frenchy's none-too-pleased teammates realized he was missing and went looking for him. They found him in the clubhouse. What the heck was he doing? they wanted to know.

Frenchy wasn't sure what all the fuss was about. He had just been in the clubhouse, he said, "adjusting his sliding pads."

The next season Frenchy returned to the big leagues, joining the Brooklyn Dodgers of the National League, whose general manager, the brilliant Branch Rickey, once described him thusly: "He's either the greatest rotten third baseman in baseball or the rottenest great third baseman. He's never in between."

Frenchy played outfield too, which made him the greatest rotten outfielder in baseball or the rottenest great outfielder—take your pick. One day, for the Dodgers, he misjudged two easy fly balls in an inning, allowing runners to get on base. Then, in the same inning, he made a splendid running catch on a line drive over his head, robbing the batter of a sure hit and ending the inning.

Later, in the dugout, when the pitcher confronted him about his two errors, Frenchy coolly replied that they were just "decoys" to trick the other team into thinking they could hit the ball over his head.

Casey Stengel's first managing job in the big leagues came with Brooklyn in 1934, the same year Frenchy joined the team. Frenchy drove him nuts. After getting a double, he was standing on second base with one foot on the dirt and the other on the bag, tapping nervously.

The second baseman asked Frenchy to lift up the foot on the bag, and Frenchy said no problem. With both his feet off the bag, the second baseman tagged him out.

An exasperated Stengel asked him how he had been tagged out while standing on the bag.

"He got me between taps," said Frenchy.

★　★　★

The Dodgers of this era were known as the Daffiness Boys, and Frenchy was one of the reasons why. One year he reported to spring training wearing a mustache and a Vandyke beard, which was unheard of at the time for ballplayers. They were nearly always clean-shaven, and somebody with hair on his face was considered very odd. So Casey ordered Frenchy to shave it off, explaining, "If there is going to be a clown on this ball club, I'm going to be it."

Frenchy enjoyed a good smoke. On a close play at second base he did not slide, coming in standing up. The fielder tagged him out. A reporter later asked him why he didn't hit the dirt.

"Because I didn't want to break the cigars in my pocket," he said.

One time, while playing the outfield, Frenchy was in hot pursuit of a fly ball. As he was running, his cap flew off his head. Frenchy stopped, turned around and got his cap, put it back on, then resumed chasing the ball.

Frenchy was such a colorful figure that sportswriters could not help putting words in his mouth, making up funny quotes that he supposedly said. Frenchy may or may not have said the following, but it's too good of a story to pass up:

Furious with a call that went against him, Frenchy spit in an umpire's face while arguing with him. For this he received a $500 fine.

"Maybe I did wrong," he reportedly said upon being informed of the fine, "but the penalty is a little more than I expectorated."

Dave Bresnahan

You will not find Dave Bresnahan's name in the *Baseball Encyclopedia*. The reason is that Bresnahan never made the major leagues, playing three seasons in the mid-1980s for a collection of low-level minor league teams.

Bresnahan's last stop in pro baseball was in Williamsport, Pennsylvania, the site of the annual Little League World Series. He was playing for Williamsport's Class A New York–Penn League club, which calls itself the Crosscutters. The Crosscutters were getting clobbered that season—they were 27 games out of first place—when their catcher decided to have a little fun.

Explaining to the home-plate ump that he needed to repair something with his glove, Bresnahan called time and ran into the Crosscutter dugout, where he grabbed a potato he had peeled earlier. Hiding the spud in his glove (which had nothing wrong with it), he ran back onto the field and the game resumed.

The pitcher pitched the next pitch, and Bresnahan caught it. The batting team had a man on third taking a lead off the bag. Bresnahan stood and deliberately fired the potato over the head of his third baseman as the runner slid back into the bag. Seeing what he thought was the ball flying over the head of the fielder, the runner got up and raced home, where the clever Bresnahan was waiting with the real ball to tag him out.

Confusion followed. Nobody except Bresnahan was quite sure what had happened. When people finally figured it out—that what everyone thought was a ball was actually a potato, and that the Crosscutters' catcher held the real ball in his glove the whole time—both teams got into a fight. The umps ultimately disallowed Bresnahan's trick and credited the opposing team with a run.

If you screw around in baseball and you've got a lot of talent, people in the game will probably look the other way. They'll say something like, "Oh well, boys will be boys," and leave it at that. But if you screw around and you've got only marginal talent, people tend to be less forgiving. Williamsport cut Bresnahan loose the day after his stunt and he never played a day of paid baseball again.

Jack Buck

In his first year of broadcasting for the St. Louis Cardinals, Jack Buck called a game in which Stan Musial hit five home runs in a May doubleheader. "My God," said the wide-eyed 29-year-old announcer. "Does he do this every Sunday?"

In his later years Buck explained that, no, the great Cardinal outfielder did not hit five home runs every Sunday, but "he did something every Sunday."

Back in those days, Buck was not yet the Voice of the Cardinals, as he would become; he was only the third man in the booth behind Milo Hamilton and lead announcer Harry Caray. Eventually, Buck became the No. 2 man behind Caray, and when Harry left the Cardinals in the late sixties, Jack took over his slot (with ex–St. Louis third baseman Mike Shannon moving in as Buck's partner in the booth). Whereas Caray was a showman, Buck was more low-key: simple, direct, even pure in his affection for the Cardinals and the game.

"That's a goner," he'd say as a home-run ball cleared the fence. Or what every St. Louis fan wanted to hear him say after the last out of a game: "That's a winner!"

Buck's broadcasts were heard on KMOX in St. Louis, the Cardinals' flagship station. With its network of stations in at least 11 states, Cardinals games could be heard around the Midwest, as well as in the South and the West, particularly at night, when the KMOX signal came in strongest. Generations of fans grew up listening to Buck's soothing, reassuring voice.

One of those was a St. Louis kid named Jerry Trupiano. It was Trupiano's dream to become a baseball broadcaster like Buck, and when he was a student at St. Louis University going to games at Busch Stadium, he would bring a large, bulky tape recorder that, as Trupiano recalls, must have weighed 45 pounds. The recorder had a microphone, and Trupiano would talk into the mic, describing the events taking place on the field as if he were announcing the game on the radio. Over time he came to know the man who was actually announcing the game, and Buck let him sit in the auxiliary press box at Busch so he could have a better view of the proceedings.

Buck listened to the youngster's tapes. He said he liked his enthusiasm and enjoyed hearing the excitement in Trupiano's voice. "Be yourself," he told him. "The listening audience will know if you're a phony."

Trupiano learned his lessons well, and is now a radio announcer for the Boston Red Sox.

Another baseball broadcaster influenced by Buck was John Rooney of the Chicago White Sox. Rooney's first-ever major league assignment was for the Cardinals. It was August, one of the team's regular announcers was absent for the day, and Rooney, hoping to make an impression, was giving it everything he had.

"Here I am," he recalls, "I'm hyped up. It was like I was calling the Final Four. I'm rapid-firing my play-by-play."

Finally, the older and wiser Buck, who was in the booth that day, says to him, "Kid, you better slow down. You're going to wear them out in a week, and you've got to be out there for 162."

The 1985 National League Championship Series between the Cardinals and Dodgers was tied at two games apiece. Entering the bottom of the ninth of Game 5 in St. Louis, the score was also knotted at two. Up to the plate came the switch-hitting Ozzie Smith to face Dodgers right-hander Tom Niedenfuer. The skinny, light-hitting fielding whiz seldom hit home runs (only 28 in 19 major league seasons), and on those rare occasions when he did hit one, it always came on a right-handed swing. He had never hit a home run left-handed—never until that moment.

For the first and only time in his career, Ozzie hit a left-handed home run, winning the game for the Cardinals and putting them ahead, 3 games to 2, in a Series they clinched two nights later. As nearly 54,000 fans at Busch Stadium went wild, Jack Buck's radio call captured the feeling of the hometown fans: "Go crazy, folks! Go crazy!"

(Of course, many people will remember another famous Buck call, this one in the Dodgers' favor: "Unbelievable!" he proclaimed after the badly injured Kirk Gibson hit a game-winning home run off the A's in the bottom of the ninth of the first game of the '88 World Series. "The Dodgers have won the game on a home run by Kirk Gibson. I don't believe what I just saw!")

John Rooney, Hall of Fame catcher Johnny Bench, and Buck were covering the '89 Athletics–Giants World Series for CBS Radio. The A's had won the first two games in Oakland, and the Series had shifted across the Bay for the next two at Candlestick Park in San Francisco when, only moments before game time, the Loma Prieta Earthquake struck the Bay Area.

The stadium, packed with more than 60,000 fans, shook under the tremors (but, fortunately, held). After the shaking stopped and they came back on the air, Buck joked to Bench, "Now, Johnny, if you'd run as fast when you played as when you got out of the booth just now, you would've never hit into a double play."

Then, explaining what it felt like to be in an earthquake, Buck told his listeners, "I thought my socks were on too tight."

When Mark McGwire hit No. 61 in 1998, tying Roger Maris's single-season home-run mark, Buck told his listening audience, "Pardon me while I stand and applaud." Then he stood up and applauded.

Chip Caray, the grandson of Harry, who is now broadcasting for the Cubs, was applying for a broadcasting job with the Cardinals a few years ago. Sitting in a hotel lobby in Pittsburgh, he was reading a newspaper, "scared to death," as he recalls, about his upcoming interview with the team. Suddenly, a quarter landed on his newspaper.

He looked up and it was Jack Buck, who had tossed it on the paper to get his attention. "Good luck," Jack said, patting Chip on the back to reassure him. "I hope everything goes well."

Smiling, Buck added, "By the way, don't screw it up."

"I had somebody say to me, 'Stan Musial is the greatest Cardinal of them all,'" Marty Brennaman, the Reds announcer, was saying. "And I said, 'No, he's not.' Because there are generations of people who have listened to the Cardinals who don't even know who Stan Musial is. They know who Jack Buck is."

Afflicted with Parkinson's disease late in life, Buck's hands trembled uncontrollably. Many of his listeners did not know this because they could not see him, but those who worked with him in the broadcast booth could not help but be aware. But Buck's style was to put people at ease by making a joking reference to it: "Hey, guys," he'd say as he entered a room, "what's shaking besides me?"

Buck, the consummate banquet speaker and storyteller, noted that Muhammad Ali also suffers from Parkinson's.

"I shook hands with Muhammad Ali recently," he told one audience. "It took them 30 minutes to get us untangled."

Another of Buck's laugh lines involved his fondness for women of Italian descent: "During World War II, an Italian woman hid me in her basement for three months. Of course, this was in Cleveland."

When terrorists attacked America on September 11, 2001, Major League Baseball stopped its games for six days. When the games resumed on September 17, Buck, a World War II vet seriously wounded in combat who received a Purple Heart for heroism, wrote a poem expressing his feelings and read it over the air. One stanza reads:

"War is just not our nature / We won't start . . . but we will end the fight / If we are involved we shall be resolved / To protect what we know is right."

The National Hall of Fame inducted Buck into the broadcasters' wing in 1987. In his induction speech, he said he could not believe how "a dirty-necked kid from Holyoke, Massachusetts," could be honored among the game's elite, telling people at Cooperstown:

"In the back here, in the library, is a plaque which says, 'Jack Buck 1924,' which is my year of birth, 'dash, and then a blank.' It's very difficult for me to look at that plaque. When I go home, I am going to send to the Hall of Fame, to Ed Stack, the figures 2020 and they can put it up there: 1924–2020. So that when I die at the age of 95, the folks can say that loudmouth finally went and now the Cardinals can hire a nice young announcer to do the work. I will be 95 at the time."

Buck did not make it to 95 as he wished. He died in 2002 at the age of 77.

Stanley Burrell

When Rickey Henderson was starring on the baseball and football teams at Oakland Tech High—as a kid, Rickey loved football even more than baseball—one of his best friends was a guy named Louis Burrell. They played ball and hung out together, and sometimes Louis's little brother, Stanley, tagged along with them. Stanley wasn't much of a ballplayer, but he loved music and dancing and was fun to be around.

"He wasn't much of an athlete," remembers Rickey. "He was into other things. He'd always carry a radio and listen to music. He'd dance, he'd sing."

Growing up in Oakland, Rickey and the Burrell brothers would go to watch the Athletics play at the Coliseum, and the way Rickey heard the story—he didn't actually *see* it, but he knew how it happened—was that one day Stanley was entertaining a group of fans in the Coliseum parking lot. Not inside the stadium, mind you, but outside in the parking lot as fans were arriving for that day's game.

As it happened, Charlie O. Finley, the owner of the Oakland franchise, walked past where Stanley was dancing and singing to the music coming out of his boom box. On the surface, at least, the two would appear to have nothing in common. Finley was a white man in his fifties; Burrell, a skinny black teenager. Finley was a Chicago-based businessman worth millions; Burrell came from a working-class family in the inner city. Finley was bald; Burrell had lots of hair.

But Finley, noticing the crowd hanging around the kid, stopped to listen and watch. And he found he enjoyed Stanley's performance so much that he invited him up to his box to watch the game. Louis Burrell's kid brother said yes, and a most unlikely friendship began.

Rickey Henderson described Stanley as Finley's "right-hand man," but this might be a bit of a reach. Burrell was more of a gofer, running errands and doing minor administrative tasks. Finley, the prototypical absentee owner, seldom came to Oakland, preferring to stay in Illinois, where his primary businesses were headquartered. But he needed a man on the scene he could trust, and this was where Stanley came in.

Sometimes Finley would call him from Chicago to give him the A's' starting lineup for the day. Burrell, seated in the owner's box at the Coliseum, would then run the lineup down to the A's manager. After the game, Burrell would call Finley to tell him the score and what happened in the game.

Lots of people in baseball (including his players) detested Finley, who had a prickly personality. He could be arrogant and insulting to the people who worked for him. But he apparently had a soft spot for Stanley, who walked around proudly wearing a cap with the initials "VP" on it. Stanley may have, in fact, been the A's' vice president, as his boss, a chronic penny-pincher, had fired or let go most everyone else in the Oakland front office at the time.

Being privy to the activities in both the A's' clubhouse and the owner's box, Stanley could share some good gossip with his brother and Rickey Henderson. He could always clue them in on the latest feuds, mostly things that the tyrannical Finley (a newspaper columnist once described him as "a self-made man who worships his creator") had said or done to anger his manager and players.

Amid all this fussin' and feudin', Stanley tried not to take sides, staying on good terms with both the owner and the ballplayers he came to know as friends. Eventually he left the A's, but two players on the club, pitcher Mike Davis and outfielder Dwayne Murphy, loaned him some money so he could cut his first record. Stanley had kept dancing and singing, and Davis and Murphy could see he had real talent and wanted to help him get started in the music business.

That first record did not sell much, but a later one did. In 1990, Stanley Burrell, operating under his new rap name of MC Hammer, or just Hammer, released a phenomenally popular CD called *Please Hammer Don't Hurt 'Em,* with the dance hits "Here Comes the Hammer" and "U Can't Touch This."

"U Can't Touch This" became the theme song of Athletics pitcher Dave Stewart (an Oakland native himself). Whenever Stewart pitched at the Coliseum, loudspeakers blasted out the song as he walked to the mound to start the game. And in 1991, at the height of Hammer's fame, he sent a huge cake to his old friend Rickey Henderson when Rickey stole his 939th base, breaking Lou Brock's career base-stealing mark to become the all-time stolen-base leader. The cake had yellow carnations on it shaped like a base.

George W. Bush

Being from an athletic family—his great-grandfather George Herbert Walker founded the Walker Cup, the international amateur golf competition; his grandfather Prescott Bush served as head of the United States Golf Association; and his father, George H. W. Bush, played first base on two national collegiate runner-up championship teams at Yale—it seems only natural that George W. Bush would be into sports, too.

Growing up in Midland in western Texas, George W.'s favorite sport was baseball. He played catcher in Little League and collected baseball cards and autographs. He would send blank index cards to his favorite players, asking for their autograph and enclosing a self-addressed, stamped envelope for their reply. Young George apparently collected quite a few signed cards before his mother, thinking they were worthless, threw them away. Barbara Bush jokes that her son still hasn't forgiven her for that.

His love of baseball following him into adulthood, George W. Bush became a partner in the ownership group that purchased the Texas Rangers in 1989. Unlike some owners, though, he was not a shadowy presence seldom seen by the fans. "He'd sit out at the old ballpark in Arlington, right beside the dugout, wearing his Rangers hat, not like the luxury-box bean counters who run the franchises now," recalls Frank Luksa, a longtime sports columnist in the Dallas–Fort Worth area. "He'd take a lot of heckling from the drunks in the stands, inviting them down to his seats to talk ball."

Bush's ownership group made Refugio, Texas, native Nolan Ryan a Ranger, which led to one of the happiest moments George W. has ever had as a baseball fan. He was sitting in the stands at old Texas Stadium, watching the Rangers play the White Sox, when Ryan threw a high, hard one close to the chin of Robin Ventura, who took offense at this, dropped his bat, and charged the mound.

"Ventura must have been out of his mind," George W. said with a grin, looking back on this moment. "Nolan cleaned his clock."

Bush eventually became governor of Texas and sold his stake in the Rangers, later deciding to run for president of the United States. On the campaign trail in New Hampshire, site of the first primary in the 2000 election, George W. carried with him a book of aphorisms by Yogi Berra. He joked that he wished he could hire Yogi as his press secretary, because, after Bush made a speaking blunder, he could then have Yogi say on his behalf, "He didn't really say everything he said."

Less than five months after becoming president, Bush instituted what he hoped would become a monthly spring and summer pastime: T-ball games on the South Lawn of the White House.

The first T-ball game, which took place in May 2001, featured boys and girls between the ages of five and eight hitting off a batting tee rather than from live pitching, as in regular baseball. "One runner had trouble finding third base," reports Frank Bruni of the *New York Times*. "Errors abounded. No official score was kept. And most of the players were under five feet tall, with a few who barely topped four feet."

Nevertheless, "the nation's baseball fanatic-in-chief" (Bruni's term) seemed pleased by what he saw. He, his wife Laura, former Red Sox star Nomar Garciaparra (then nursing an injury and unable to play), broadcaster Bob Costas, and many others all laughed heartily as the Famous Chicken stuck a baseball down the mouth of his costume and then had two balls drop out of his butt.

Presidents have been throwing out first pitches since the days of William Taft in the early 1900s, but no presidential pitch has ever had as much drama—or been attended by so much security—as the ceremonial first ball thrown by Bush at Game 3 of the 2001 World Series at Yankee Stadium, the first major sporting event in New York after the attacks on the World Trade Center. As baseball writer Roger Angell noted, Bush stood on the mound and from the full distance threw the ball to Yankees catcher Jorge Posada.

Perhaps drawing from the book of aphorisms he carried with him while running for president, President Bush quoted Yogi Berra in his 2002 State of the Union address: "If you come to a fork in the road," he said, referring to an initiative he was proposing, "take it."

Bush is not the only person from his administration with a fondness for the game. Former White House press secretary Ari Fleischer is a Yankees fan who, after 9/11, used code names when he traveled on presidential business to Florida. When people wanted to reach him at the hotel where he was staying, they asked for him not by his name but that of Bernie Williams, the Yankees outfielder.

Asked by a reporter why Fleischer chose Williams over some

other Yankee, he said, "Derek Jeter is too obvious, and [ex-Yankee] Alfonso Soriano is not credible, which is why I went for Bernie Williams."

When this reporter proposed Yankees owner George Steinbrenner as a possible pseudonym, Fleischer said, "The whole purpose is not to become a target."

President George W. Bush has thrown out the ceremonial first pitch on three occasions: the World Series at Yankee Stadium, before the inaugural game at new Miller Park in Milwaukee, and Opening Day for the 2004 season at Busch Stadium between the Cardinals and Brewers. Naturally, security was extremely tight at all three venues. In St. Louis, hundreds of uniformed and plainclothed police officers and federal agents staked out positions in and around Busch Stadium, including on the roof scanning the crowd with binoculars. Some agents posed as ballpark ushers, donning usher uniforms. Secret Service agent Brian Piersall put on a Brewers uniform and stood inside the Milwaukee dugout as if he were a member of the team.

Piersall, who wasn't even a baseball fan, asked one of the Brewers players what he should do if spectators asked for his autograph.

"Just sign," said the player.

As at Yankee Stadium and Miller Park, the Bush visit to Busch Stadium proceeded without incident.

Harry Caray

Many people think Harry Caray broadcasted only baseball, and only for the Chicago Cubs, but in his more than 40 years behind the microphone he covered several different teams besides the Cubs and more sports than just baseball. Way back in the 1960s, when Harry was calling the games for the St. Louis (now Atlanta) Hawks of the National Basketball Association, he had just checked into a Memphis hotel room when the phone rang.

Harry picked it up. On the other end was the husky-throated voice of a man.

"Harry," said the man. "I been listening to ya for years." The voice sounded familiar—it had a slight twang—but Harry couldn't quite place it. "How are the Cardinals gonna do this season?"

Besides the Hawks, Harry was also broadcasting the St. Louis Cardinals, the first major league club he worked for. "I think we're gonna be okay," Harry said. "We've got a good ball club. Who is this?"

"Elvis," said the man.

"Elvis who?" asked Harry.

"Elvis Presley."

"Don't give me that," said Harry, who thought someone was pulling a practical joke on him. "You're not Elvis Presley."

But the man who claimed to be the king of rock 'n' roll challenged Harry to be in the hotel lobby in ten minutes. Harry took the challenge, and at the appointed time, a big Cadillac rolled up in front of the hotel. Inside was Elvis—the real one, not an impostor.

The two then drove off to Graceland for an afternoon of talking baseball and listening to music, until it was time for Harry to leave for the Hawks game, which was being played that night in Memphis. When the game ended, the big Caddy was waiting outside the arena to bring Harry back to Elvis's place, and the two future legends ate barbecued ribs and drank Bud well into the night.

The composer Albert Von Tilzer and the lyricist Jack Norworth wrote the baseball anthem "Take Me Out to the Ballgame" in 1908. But it was not until Harry Christopher Carabina (Harry's birth name; he was of French-Romanian and Italian stock) began singing it for the Chicago White Sox that the song came to be such a standard part of going to a ball game.

The year was 1976. After a quarter-century with the Cardinals and one with the Oakland Athletics, Caray, who was anywhere from 54 to 62 years old (no one is quite sure when he was born), had been with the White Sox about five years. The White Sox owner was Bill Veeck, a longtime baseball man who had just purchased the club. A genius at promotion, who had once hired a midget to bat for one of his teams, Veeck happened to see Harry singing "Take Me Out to the Ballgame" in the radio booth as the crowd was singing the song during the seventh-inning stretch on Opening Day at Comiskey Park in Chicago.

This gave Veeck an idea. Why not turn on the microphone when Harry was singing and let the fans hear him? So the next day Veeck did just that. Only he didn't tell Harry, who, much to his surprise, found his off-key singing broadcast all over the park.

When Harry approached Veeck about it, Veeck explained his reasoning: "Anybody in the ballpark hearing you sing that song knows he can sing as well as you can. Probably better. So he or she is going to sing along with you."

And so it came to pass. From that day on, for the rest of his seasons with the White Sox and for the sixteen after that with the Cubs, Harry led the hometown fans in famously off-key renditions of "Take Me Out to the Ballgame."

★   ★   ★

With his gravelly voice ("Hello again, everybody. Harry Caray here on a beautiful day for baseball"), white hair, and large-framed black glasses, Harry was nearly as popular in Chicago as the song he loved to sing. Asked once what he was going to do when he retired, Harry said, "Never." He died in the spring of 1998, just before the start of another Cubs season.

Sean Casey

When Sean Casey was still a teenager, he got caught stealing Ken Griffey, Jr., baseball cards at a card shop in his hometown of Upper St. Clair, Pennsylvania. Junior was a rookie that year, breaking in with the Seattle Mariners. He has since moved over to Cincinnati, where one of his teammates on the Reds is the grown-up Sean Casey.

That shoplifting incident made a lasting impression on Casey, whose father took him aside after it happened and began reading from a dictionary. He chose certain words in the dictionary and read their definitions to his son. A few of the words he read were: *greed, selfish, trust.*

"The lesson I got was that life isn't just about you and the things you want," says Sean. "You need to think about other people."

No. 21 on the Reds, with brown hair, a goatee, and a broad smile, Casey is by all accounts one of the world's nicest guys. (A local chapter of the Baseball Writers Association of America, in fact, gave him a Good Guy Award one year.) Early in his career, Mike Kirby, a minor league manager, dubbed him "The Mayor" because of the way Sean likes to socialize with just about everybody he sees—the ump and catcher when he comes to the plate to hit, runners at first base when he's playing the field, his teammates, opposing players, fans.

The year Kirby managed him in the Cape Cod League, Casey was signing autographs after a game and started talking to a family that lived in the area. The family became so enamored of The Mayor that they invited him back to their house for dinner and even let him drive their Buick Regal around town.

A few days later, Kirby was on his way to the park for a game when he spotted Casey waving to him from the side of the road. He was standing next to the Buick, which had run out of gas.

Kirby pulled over and got the story: "Coach," Sean explained, "I thought this car was getting the best mileage. I drove it for three days and it still had half a tank of gas. I just found out the gas gauge is broken."

Pitcher Danny Graves has been a teammate of Casey's for years. Beginning in '97, they played together in Buffalo (American Association), Cleveland (majors), Indianapolis (International League), and back to the majors in Cincinnati. On one of their stops, Graves gave Casey a pair of spikes—the first free pair Sean received.

"Seriously," Danny was saying, "he thanks me for them all the time. 'I wouldn't be hitting .370 today if it weren't for those free spikes,' he says. And the thing is, they weren't even his size."

Besides being a nice guy and a big, lefty swinger who can powder the ball into the outfield gaps, Casey hates to spend money, even though he's now making millions in the game. "Cheap" is a word that friends use to describe him, with affection. "You just hate to go to lunch with him," says teammate Adam Dunn, "because you know who's going to wind up paying." Not Sean.

Casey is always borrowing Dunn's and other guys' cell phones, because he doesn't want to pay for one of his own. He's not into fashion—jeans and sweatshirts are the norm—and although he's taken a step up from that old Buick Regal with the broken gas gauge, his current vehicle is a ten-year-old Honda Accord.

One spring he tried to pull the Accord into the players' parking lot at the Reds' training camp in Sarasota. The security guard working the lot wouldn't let him in because he couldn't believe that a major league ballplayer would be driving a car that old.

"This lot is for players only," he said.

"I'm a player," Sean protested.

"You're a player?" said the guard. "What are you driving this thing for?"

The guard eventually relented and let him park there. Casey, who still sleeps in his old bedroom in his parents' house in Upper St. Clair when the Reds travel to play Pittsburgh, swears he's going to hang on to that car as long as it keeps running.

Roger Clemens

For much of Roger Clemens's career, people criticized him as a guy who couldn't pitch under pressure, who couldn't win the big game. But these people may forget that Clemens, an All-State baseball player at Spring Woods High in Texas, an All-American at San Jacinto Junior College, and a two-time All-American at the University of Texas, started and won the final game of the 1983 College World Series, beating Alabama 4 to 3 to claim the national collegiate championship for the Longhorns.

Roger's nickname is "The Rocket," and anyone who has played with him or batted against him knows why. He pitches *mad*. "Everyone kind of perceives me as being angry," he said once. "It's not anger. It's motivation." Okay, then. He pitches motivated.

One of his most motivated pitching performances came on April 29, 1986, in a night game between the Boston Red Sox and Seattle Mariners. Showing that he was fully healed from shoulder surgery the previous year, Clemens struck out all three Mariners batters in the first inning. Then he struck out the side again in both the fourth and fifth innings. As the strikeouts mounted—two more in the sixth, two more in the seventh, two more in the eighth—fans posted "K" signs in the right-field seats at Fenway Park. Fans put up the 20th and final K after Phil Bradley of the Mariners went down on a called third strike in the ninth.

The 24-year-old Clemens became the first pitcher in baseball history to strike out 20 batters in a regulation nine-inning game. And he did so without issuing a walk. At the time of his first pitch, about 7,000 fans were at Fenway. But as news of what was going on in the game spread around Boston, another 6,000 people showed up to watch. The official paid attendance jumped to more than 13,000, setting a Red Sox record for most people to buy tickets while a game was in progress.

That 1986 season remains a bitter memory for Red Sox fans, at least the way it ended. After being one out away from winning the world championship, Boston lost Game 6 (and then, two nights later, Game 7) of the World Series to the New York Mets. In that fateful Game 6, Red Sox reliever Calvin Schiraldi entered in the eighth inning with Boston leading 3 to 2. He was replacing the Sox starter, who could no longer continue because of a blister on his finger. That starter was Roger Clemens.

Clemens won 24 games with only four losses and a 2.48 earned run average for the Red Sox in 1986, collecting both the Cy Young and Most Valuable Player trophies. After this feat, Hank Aaron said he did not think pitchers should be named MVP. Pitchers have their award, the Cy Young, and only everyday players should be eligible for the MVP, he said.

To which Roger responded, "I wish [Hank] was still playing. I'd probably crack his head open to show him how valuable I was."

Unfairly or not, Clemens developed a reputation for failing to perform under pressure. His detractors pointed not only to Game 6 in '86 but to Game 4 in 1990 of the American League Championship Series against the Athletics. In the first game of that Series, Dave Stewart of the A's, known as a money pitcher, beat Clemens and the Red Sox easily. After Oakland won the next two games, Stewart and Clemens were set to face off again. Some Clemens critics claimed he was scared to pitch against his Oakland counterpart because he knew he could not beat the stronger A's.

Clemens took the mound in the bottom of the first inning wearing eye black, a black paste applied to the skin underneath the eyes to reduce the sun's glare. It is usually worn only by infielders or outfielders, not pitchers—a fact Clemens admitted after the game. He was wearing it, he said, not for protection against the sun but as part of his game face. He was going into battle dressed in war paint.

The battle didn't last long. Clemens, perhaps *too* psyched up for his version of baseball combat, got thrown out in the second inning for arguing with the home-plate ump. The A's went on to win the game and move on to the World Series.

Clemens's most notorious confrontation—he's had a few in his time—came in 2000, the year after he joined the Yankees. In an interleague game against the crosstown Mets, he nailed Mike Piazza with a fastball to the head. Fortunately, Piazza was wearing a helmet; otherwise, the leading home-run-hitting catcher of all time might have been hurt even more seriously than the concussion he suffered.

But the beaning begat renewed criticism of Clemens, who was attacked as a headhunter. Even so, The Rocket remained defiant. In order to pitch successfully in the big leagues, he has said many times, you have to go inside on hitters.

"If I'm going to miss, I'm going to miss in somebody's shirt or in the other batter's box. It's their job to get out of the way."

Act Two in the Roger Clemens–Mike Piazza drama came in the Subway World Series later in the year. In the first inning of Game 2, with Piazza at the plate and Clemens facing him, a Clemens fastball broke Piazza's bat and sheared it into pieces as he swung. The head of the bat landed near the feet of Clemens, who, strangely, inexplicably, even . . . *crazily*, picked it up and threw it at Piazza as Mike ran down the first-base line.

Piazza stepped toward Clemens and started shouting at him as both benches cleared. "I asked him what his problem was, basically," said Piazza. "I was trying to figure out if it was intentional or not."

Nobody was quite sure why Roger did what he did, including Roger. "It was just a reaction all of a sudden," he said afterward. "I was extremely emotional in the first inning. I had no idea Mike ran. There was no [malicious] intent."

The Mets weren't so sure. "Some of the guys thought he threw it at Mike," said Mets manager Bobby Valentine. John Franco was one of those guys: "I think he knew what he was doing all along, but I'm sure he's going to come up with an excuse again. Just like last time. I think a lot of our guys lost respect for him for what he did."

Lots of outraged Mets fans (Piazza was, and is, popular in New York) called for Clemens to receive the same kind of treatment he was so fond of dishing out. It took two years before Clemens would finally come to bat against the Mets. Although the two teams had faced off since the 2000 World Series, the Yankee pitching rotation always managed to keep Clemens away from Shea Stadium, the home of the Mets. The job of drilling Clemens fell to Mets left-hander Shawn Estes, who delivered a fastball a foot or two behind

Roger's butt. As a message pitch designed to scare the then six-time Cy Young winner into changing his ways, it left something to be desired. Nevertheless, Estes delivered perhaps the best message of all, hitting a two-run homer off Clemens and pitching seven shutout innings in an 8 to 0 Mets laugher. Piazza also hit a homer, though not against his arch-nemesis.

Having passed the age of 40 and played on a pair of world championship teams with the Yankees, restoring his reputation as a pitcher able to produce under pressure, Clemens announced that 2003 would be his last season in the majors. In honor of his distinguished career, he received parting gifts from the Yankees and standing ovations not only at Yankee Stadium but at parks around the American League where the Yankees were visiting.

But in the off-season Roger changed his mind and un-retired, signing a deal with his hometown Houston Astros to pitch in 2004; he would go on to win his seventy Cy Young Award. Derek Jeter, his former Yankees teammate, cracked, "He owes us a Hummer. We gave him a Hummer for retiring, and he didn't give it back."

Pitching for Houston, Clemens threw a supercharged fastball that a hitter fouled off. The umpire tossed Clemens a new ball, which, upon inspection, he returned to the ump. He apparently didn't like the feel of that ball, and the ump gave him another one.

Seeing Clemens toss the first ball back, the batter figured that Clemens was asking for a ball that gave him a better grip. This likely meant his next pitch was going to be a curveball.

This is exactly what Clemens wanted the batter to think and why he asked for a new ball: To put the possibility of a curve in the batter's mind. On the next pitch, Clemens unloosed another fastball, even faster than the one before, and struck the man out looking.

His teammates in Houston called it the "Rocket Hole"—that place down at the far end of the dugout at Minute Maid Park where

Clemens stood during the bottom half of the inning when the Astros were up and he wasn't pitching. The Rocket cheered and yelled with such intensity that his teammates did not venture near the Rocket Hole during a game. One of those who stayed away was Brad Ausmus, explaining, "I don't know if it's safe to go by him or not."

Clemens's sons all play youth baseball, and Clemens often attends games and helps out with their teams. When a reporter told Jeff Bagwell of the Astros that he saw Roger pitch against eight- and nine-year-olds in a Midget baseball league in Houston, Bagwell replied, "Oh yeah? How many did he knock down?"

In the 2004 All-Star Game in Houston, Roger Clemens started for the National League. His catcher was Mike Piazza. The two played together without incident, though Clemens's old friends in the American League treated him unkindly, scoring six runs off him in the first inning. While the emotionally intense Clemens was being pounded by opposing hitters, Piazza remained behind home plate and did not go out to the mound to settle him down.

Coors Field

Strange things happen at Coors Field, and they began happening in the very first major league game ever played there, April 26, 1995, between the Colorado Rockies and the New York Mets. The first batter up for the Mets, Brett Butler, got a base hit, though he failed to score. The first run ever scored at Coors came in the home half of the first, Larry Walker knocking in Walt Weiss. Walker's double was the first extra-base hit in Coors history. Rico Brogna of the Mets struck the first-ever home run, in the fourth, and in that same inning teammate Todd Hundley produced the first-ever grand slam. The teams kept slugging and the game went into extra innings, the Rockies winning on a Dante Bichette three-run jack in the fourteenth. Final score: Rockies 11, Mets 9.

An 11 to 9 score may not seem strange to hitters. They may consider that just another day at the office, a day in which they were simply seeing the ball really, really well. Pitchers tend to view things from a different perspective. For them, a game in which 20 total runs are scored is a freak of nature. But that's Coors Field for you. For hitters and fans, it's a joy; for pitchers, a horror show.

The reason Coors causes such dread among pitchers is, of course, its mile-high elevation. Pitched balls behave differently there than they do at sea level. Curves tend to curve less because the thin mountain air offers less resistance, and while fastballs may get to the plate a little faster, they do not tend to move around as much. Hungry hitters can feed off these straighter fastballs and noncurving curves.

Scientists calculate (Coors Field is a place where the calculations of scientists must be considered) that a batted ball flies approximately 9 percent farther in Denver than it does at sea level. So if a ball travels 400 feet at Yankee Stadium, if struck equally hard at Coors it would fly about 436 feet. The distance to the fences at Coors Field are 347 feet in left, 390 in left center, 415 in straightaway center, 375 in right center, and 350 in right. When a Colorado player hits a home run, water fountains in center shoot off. Needless to say, the fountains shoot off frequently.

Many Colorado baseball fans are sensitive about their ballpark's reputation. They would prefer to talk about the majestic views of the

Rocky Mountains that can be seen from some of its seats and the park's other lovely features. All out-of-towners can talk about, though, is its reputation as a baseball version of Hitsville, USA.

"It's regarded as the weirdest ballpark in the majors," sports columnist Bill Gallo was saying the year after Coors made its major league debut, "where tattered journeyman batters are transformed into supermen, where visiting pitchers must confer with their psychotherapists, and where banjo hitters park their bloopers in the cheap seats."

Still, local sensitivities aside, it's hard to argue with the numbers. In one three-game series against the Mets in '96, the scores were 10 to 7, 11 to 10, and 7 to 6. Batters hit safely 87 times with 12 home runs. At one point in the season, the Rockies were hitting .344 as a team and scoring eight runs per game at home; on the road, these figures were .223 and a little over two.

On the road, Gallo joked, opposing pitchers could throw a basketball by Vinny Castilla. But in the elevated climes of Coors Field, he, Dante Bichette, Larry Walker, and Todd Helton (after he joined the team in '98 for his first full season) came to be known as the Blake Street Bombers for their slugging exploits.

The Rockies traditionally lead the National League in team batting, slugging percentage, and other hitting categories. Visiting batters also perform exceptionally well there. In 1998, on his way to 66 for the season, Sammy Sosa hit four home runs in two games at Coors Field and added 14 runs batted in for good measure.

You can count on Coors Field to be the highest-scoring park in the majors. In 1999, the average score of a game there was 8 to 7. Good for fans who love seeing lots of men crossing home plate, not so good for pitchers and their managers trying to avoid burning up all the available arms on their staff. The Rockies lost one 1999 game after leading by eight runs. In another game, nine different players on Colorado and Seattle hit home runs, tying a record for the number of players to hit homers in a single game. The Rockies and visiting clubs clocked 303 home runs that year, the most home runs ever for a season in a major league park.

Seeking to turn their fortunes around and get more pitching in their hitter-heavy lineup (since their inception in '93, they have yet to win a division title), the Rockies signed lefties Denny Neagle and Mike Hampton to high-priced contracts after the 2000 season. But Coors Field wore them both down, turning them into losers, and after two seasons of failure, a grateful Hampton left town for the sea-level Atlanta Braves.

One off-season in Colorado, an electrician at Coors Field, Tony Cowell, went on a hunting trip. While tramping around in the water and mud, he noticed how moisture softened the leather on his boots. One problem faced by pitchers in the mile-high altitude is that with the lack of moisture in the air, they sometimes cannot grip the ball the way they usually do. Upon release, the ball then does not move the way they'd like it to. Cowell wondered if exposing balls to humidity would help pitchers get a better grip and thereby improve their performances. Club officials agreed it was worth a try and built the world's first climate-controlled storage chamber for baseballs at Coors Field.

In its first year, the chamber was kept at 40 degrees humidity, with the temperature controlled as well. Every month the Rockies received shipments of new balls, which they stored in the chamber until practice or game time. Although early results were promising, the humidity chamber clearly did not solve the problem. The balls kept flying. The water fountains kept shooting off.

Just ask San Diego manager Bruce Bochy. After the Padres took a 9 to 7 lead over the Rockies going into the bottom of the ninth, only to lose, he calmly addressed reporters in the clubhouse afterward. Then, when he was done, he kicked over a water cooler and screamed, "I hate this place!"

★   ★   ★

The Giants experienced a similar fate early one season. In the top of the ninth, after home runs by Michael Tucker and Barry Bonds, they took a 9 to 6 lead. But in the bottom half of the frame, the Rockies hit two home runs and scored four times to win 10 to 9. The result thrilled the hometown fans, suffering through yet another down year for their club, and left the Giants pitchers shaking their heads. "The ball keeps traveling, like it's growing wings," said a weary Dustin Hermanson poetically. Added Jim Brower: "It's Coors Field. It's a different place. Weird things happen."

Disco Demolition

Late in the fall of 1978, Bill Veeck, owner of the Chicago White Sox, sent a letter to White Sox season-ticket holders promising better things to come for the team. "We have, for the first time in some years, a bunch of promising young athletes," wrote Veeck, who, a month earlier, had hired Don Kessinger to be the club's new player-manager. Though short on managing experience (Kessinger, in fact, had never managed in the big leagues before), the six-time All-Star Cub shortstop was popular in Chicago and his low-key personal style seemed a good fit with the youngsters on the club.

The Opening Day lineup for the Sox that year featured 5-foot-3-inch shortstop Harry Chappas, the shortest player in the major leagues, who had made the cover of *Sports Illustrated* earlier in the spring. People made a big fuss about Harry because he was so small, and he quickly grew tired of all the unwanted attention. Indeed, he became so wary of reporters that he refused to be interviewed on tape and would check to make sure no one was taping what he said without his permission. Soon the 21-year-old, one of those promising youngsters Veeck was counting on, was sent down to the minors.

Another member of the Sox's Opening Day lineup—he batted second behind Chappas, the leadoff hitter—was left fielder Claudell Washington, who had come over from Texas during the previous season. Washington made no secret of the fact that he did not want to play for the White Sox, a perennial American League also-ran, and reported to Chicago several days late. When asked why he showed up so late, Claudell, who ultimately played 17 seasons in the big leagues, reportedly offered one of the all-time great excuses.

"I overslept," he said.

The Opening Day third baseman was Eric Soderholm, who used a hypnotist to improve his performance and tried to get his teammates to do the same. Most declined. A couple of months into the season, Soderholm took the reverse route of Claudell Washington—Chicago to Texas—and when he left the Sox he wrote a good-bye poem for his teammates: "Good-bye," it said. "It sure has been fun. Sod's off to Texas to play in the sun. But in my heart I'll always miss you."

Sod left in June, as the fortunes of the White Sox declined. Their promising youngsters did not deliver as hoped (although center fielder Chet Lemon, who batted third in the Opening Day lineup, did make the All-Star team for the second straight year), and the club's losses overwhelmed its wins. Attendance at Comiskey Park, never high, sunk. Things got so bad that Mike Veeck, Bill's son, who worked in the White Sox front office, proposed a novel promotion in order to lure fans to the ballpark. It was called "Disco Demolition Night."

★　　★　　★

Two years earlier, *Saturday Night Fever,* starring John Travolta, had its motion picture premiere. The film became a monster hit, catapulting Travolta, previously best known as Vinnie Barberino in TV's *Welcome Back, Kotter,* into superstardom. One element of the movie's success was its sound track, which included a number of songs by leading disco artists of the time, most prominently the Bee Gees. "How Deep Is Your Love" and "Staying Alive" were two No. 1 hits on that album.

Although the disco craze had cooled somewhat by 1979, the Bee Gees, Donna Summer ("Bad Girls," her classic produced by Giorgio Moroder, came out that year), Gloria Gaynor (her signature song, "I Will Survive," may be disco's unofficial anthem), and other disco artists were still selling records. This irritated the heck out of Steve Dahl, a disc jockey for WLUP-FM, who was drawing a big audience in Chicago's competitive radio market by blowing up disco records on the air.

He didn't really blow the records up; he just pretended to. But lots of people (rock fans and other disco haters, mainly) enjoyed the joke and tuned in to hear him. And so it came to pass that Mike Veeck invited him out to Comiskey Park on the night of July 12 to blow up records—for real—between games of a White Sox–Tigers doubleheader.

"I was dreading the whole thing," recalls Dahl. "It seemed to me if I drew 5,000 people, I would be parading around in a helmet and blowing up records in what looked like an empty stadium."

He need not have worried. Nearly 48,000 fans, one of the largest crowds of the season, came out to the old ballyard that night. Many of the attendees were young, long-haired, and possibly high on something other than life. Some of them climbed the walls and sneaked in. As they watched Detroit handle Chicago 4 to 1 in the first game, it was clear most of them were not there to see baseball. They had come to see disco records go up in smithereens.

★   ★   ★

In those days there was no such thing as a compact disc; record albums were made of vinyl and about the size and shape of a Frisbee, and if you held a record album with your fingers on its edge and threw it, it would fly in the air something like a Frisbee. Which was exactly what some of the anti-discoites started doing in the late innings of the first game: tossing the work of the Brothers Gibb et al. onto the field. The public address announcer at the stadium asked them to please stop, but they could hardly restrain themselves.

This was only one of many mistakes made by White Sox officials. To boost attendance for the promotion, all fans who brought a disco record with them could get into the game for only 98 cents. Ushers were supposed to collect the records when people entered the stadium, but many albums made it past these checkpoints and ended up in pieces on the field.

The surge of fans onto the playing field began shortly after Steve Dahl blew up his first disco album on a stage in center field. "It looked like medieval times when they go after a castle, pouring over a wall," said one horrified observer as the fans streamed out of the stands.

Thousands of fans poured onto the field. It was not chaos, perhaps, but something that nearly resembled it. People doused Dahl with beer and threw records and other hard objects at him. Record albums spinning through the air cut into those unfortunate enough to get in their way. Others attached M-80s to the disco albums and threw them at people. Lighted, exploding things were flying around crazily: firecrackers, cherry bombs, bottle rockets. One group of fans pushed over the batting cage parked along a fence. Others made trash fires in the infield. At one point, White Sox broadcaster Harry Caray made a fervent plea for people to leave the field and stop their mischief. None of the mischief-makers paid him any mind.

After about a half hour, Chicago's finest appeared on the field, some on horses, and cleared everyone off. All that was left of the stage in center was smoking wreckage. "It looked like a spaceship took off from center field," said Dave Phillips, one of the umpires who worked the game that night. "It was smoldering."

Considering that a near-riot had occurred and the field was littered with smoking debris, Phillips and the other umpires canceled the scheduled second game of the doubleheader. Nearly 40 people were arrested, but no one was hurt seriously; only minor scrapes and cuts were reported. After that night, Steve Dahl returned to spinning platters on Chicago radio (a gig he still enjoys). Mike Veeck resolved never to do another disco-related baseball promotion again. Don Kessinger got fired in August, never to manage again. And the promising young White Sox finished the season in the lower ranks of their division with a losing record.

Dennis Eckersley

The year was 1975. Dennis Eckersley of the Cleveland Indians was looking good and pitching even better. Then only 20 years old, with longish brown hair and a mustache, Eckersley was in the midst of a terrific rookie season in which he would eventually win 17 games and be named American League Rookie Pitcher of the Year.

Opposing him were the Texas Rangers, managed by Billy Martin, who sent out one of his oldest pitchers to face Eckersley in the night game at Arlington Stadium. This was in the days when the use of a radar gun to record the speed of a pitcher's pitches was still a novelty. After each delivery, an operator would post the speed of the pitch on the Arlington scoreboard for all to see.

One of those people avidly following these postings was Eckersley, who was stunned at what he was seeing. According to the scoreboard, his fastest fastball was only 85 mph, while the old-timer for the Rangers was throwing in the mid-nineties.

"There's no way that old goat is throwing harder than me," Eck said to himself, vowing to throw even harder when he went out to the mound the next inning. But it didn't do any good. His fastest pitches still registered slower on the gun than those of the aging veteran he opposed.

It was later revealed that Billy Martin, a truly crafty old goat of a manager, had arranged for the operator to post false radar-gun readings on the scoreboard in order to unnerve the young right-hander for the Indians. And it worked. Eckersley may have started throwing harder, but (to borrow the old Lefty Gomez line) the ball apparently didn't get there as fast, and the Rangers pounded him and beat the Indians easily.

Eckersley was a cocky pitcher, full of swagger, and he had no fear of getting in the face of hitters. In May 1977, his last season with the Indians, he took a no-hitter into the top of the ninth against the Angels. Pitching in front of his home fans at Cleveland Stadium, he struck out Bobby Grich and retired pinch hitter Willie Aikens on a fly ball to nail down the first two outs of the inning. Only weak-hitting rookie Gil Flores stood between him and a no-hitter.

As Flores came up to the plate, he and Eckersley both saw the crowd of photographers squeezing into a field-level box near the dugout, hoping to capture the last out of the game on film and the celebration that would surely follow.

But Flores kept stepping out of the box, delaying the game and making everyone wait. "Nobody is trying to take your picture," Eckersley finally yelled at him. "Just get in there. You're the last out."

Flores stepped back in, made the last out, and Eck had his no-hitter.

Despite his success in Cleveland (he made the All-Star team in his last year there), in 1978 Eckersley found himself in a new uniform and a new city. He quickly became a fan favorite in Boston—not only because he won 20 games for the Red Sox that year, but also because of his gift of gab. The man had a way with a phrase.

Peter Gammons, the ESPN commentator, dubbed his flair for language "Eckese." Others referred to it as "dialeckt." Whatever you called it, nobody talked baseball quite like Eck. After a game, reporters would hover around his locker, scribbling down his assessment of what had just occurred on the field.

"I knew what they wanted," he would say, describing a moment in which Fenway's fans were screaming for a strikeout. "But I didn't want to get caught up in it. If I throw him the heater, maybe he juices it out on me."

"Juices it out," in Eckese, meant "hit a home run." Another phrase for hitting a home run was "take it to the bridge." Today, a "heater" is fairly well known as a fastball; less so back then. Eckersley might have also used the term "gas" to describe his fastball. His curveball was a "hammer," "nastie," or "yakker"; when he got a batter out on a curve, Eck "yakked him out."

A strikeout was never merely a strikeout for Eckersley; it was "a punchout." When his control was sharp, his pitches skimming off the edges of the plate, Eck was "painting" the corners or throwing "in the paint." (Several of these phrases are more common today, in part because of Eckersley's influence.) In Eckese, "iron" was money and "liquor" was oil. "Bogart" was a big game, such as Opening Day or a playoff, and "salad hitters" were pushovers, easy outs. A "fossil master" was an old-timer.

Boston's fans loved Eckersley for his flair on the mound and his flair with the language, but in baseball, love affairs tend to last only as long as a player contributes to a winning team. Gradually, his contributions to the Red Sox diminished, and in 1984, Fenway's boo birds (an old-fashioned slang term, long predating Eckese) chased him away to the Cubs. He helped Chicago win the Eastern Division title that year, but two seasons later his pitching career was in flames. Salad hitters and fossil masters were juicing him out. He was a failure as a painter, and was punching nobody out. After winning 6 games and losing 11 with a 4.57 earned run average in '86, the Cubs sent him to Oakland, happy to get rid of him.

This turning point trade coincided with a turning point moment in Eckersley's personal life. The good-looking Eck had always been a party guy, a big drinker, a fast liver. "I was an animal," as he said once. During that off-season, he took his daughter over to his sister-in-law's house and then got drunk. His sister-in-law, hoping to show him how he was wrecking his life, videotaped him. The next day, a sober Eckersley watched the tape and saw how foolish he had acted, how badly he had behaved around his daughter. Later that month, he enrolled in a treatment center for alcoholism.

The Oakland Athletics knew nothing about Eckersley's alcoholism, because he did not tell them. He told no one except perhaps his immediate family, keeping the knowledge to himself even as he worked out harder than he ever had before and got in the best physical shape of his life. Though on the dark side of thirty, Eck still felt he had the goods to be a starting pitcher in the big leagues.

The A's thought differently. They felt his days as a starter were done and pegged him as a long reliever. Eckersley resisted. In those days, relieving was not dominated by high-priced specialists as it is now. The bullpen was for guys who were not good enough to make it as a starter or old-timers whose best days were in scrapbooks and highlight reels. Eckersley still thought he could be a starter.

Then Tony LaRussa, entering his first full season as A's manager, gave it to him straight. "You're not a starter on this club," Tony told him bluntly, and Eck had no choice but to take a seat in the bullpen.

★ ★ ★

One of the ways LaRussa persuaded Eckersley to accept his new, lesser role (at least in Eckersley's mind) was to tell him that the best moment for a pitcher in baseball was at the end of a game when he was shaking hands with his teammates on the field after a win. This seldom happened for a starter, because by the ninth he was usually out of the game. If Eck became a reliever, LaRussa said, he'd get a chance to shake hands with his teammates all the time.

But Eckersley did not become the closer for the A's right away. In '87, the job first belonged to hard-throwing Jay Howell. Eck took over the job only by default, stepping in when Howell got hurt. But it quickly became Eck's to keep. He recorded 16 saves that year and 45 the next. LaRussa's use of Eckersley—saving him to pitch just in the ninth inning, where it would usually be three men up, three men out—invented the modern idea of a closer. Now teams all over baseball have one guy (or wish they had one guy) who enters in the ninth with the aim of retiring the side and shutting the other team down.

Eckersley's most famous single moment in baseball was also his least glorious: the ninth-inning home run he gave up to the limping Kirk Gibson in Game 1 of the 1988 World Series between the A's and Dodgers. Gibson's homer, one of the most dramatic in Series history, beat Oakland and propelled Los Angeles to a five-game victory over the highly favored Athletics.

Asked later what Gibson's home run had taught him as a pitcher, Eckersley said flippantly, "Never throw a changeup to a cripple."

Not a day goes by that some fan he meets on the street or at the ballpark fails to mention the Gibson homer to him. "It's like the Kennedy assassination," Eckersley has said. "Everyone I see comes up and tells me where they were and what they were doing when Gibson hit that home run."

In '89, the bitterness of the previous year's Series gave way to joy. Oakland swept San Francisco to become world champions, and Eckersley pitched the final out of the final game, celebrating with his teammates on the field.

At the top of his game, Eckersley was like Mariano Rivera or Eric Gagne at their best: automatic. When he came into the game in the ninth, it usually meant only one thing: game over. His teammates and opposing hitters knew it. The radio broadcasters for the A's knew it. When Eckersley would begin warming up in the bullpen, Lon Simmons and Bill King would start organizing their notes for the postgame wrap-up. Fans knew it, too. Borrowing a page from Los Angeles Dodgers fans, who often leave in the seventh or eighth inning of a game to beat the Chavez Ravine traffic, fans at the Oakland Coliseum would start heading for their cars as soon as Eckersley appeared. They knew he was going to punch out the side 1-2-3, and the Eck Man rarely disappointed them.

Eckersley supposedly ate a turkey sandwich with mustard before every game. Never mayonnaise. The reason: Mayonnaise was fattening, he said, and he never wanted to throw a fat pitch. "Mustard" is also a longtime baseball term for a hard fastball, a fastball that really has something on it. No fat, lots of mustard: That was how the sidearm-flinging Eckersley pitched.

He was a man of many habits. The sportswriter Neil Hayes, who covered Eckersley in Oakland, explained how Eck's ritual on the day of a game was always the same. He would stay in his street clothes, hanging out in the clubhouse, until the fifth inning. Then he'd suit up and sit in the A's dugout for the sixth and seventh. In the eighth, he'd take the long walk down to the bullpen. When the bullpen phone rang telling him to get ready, he'd throw eight warm-up pitches. Never more, never less. Always eight. Then he was ready to go.

Ever the phrasemaker, good with the media—in fact, he now analyzes Red Sox games on TV—Eckersley is given credit for coining the term "walk-off home run." This term has become so popular among some people that it has almost replaced the phrase "game-winning home run," which is what a walk-off is.

Eck was referring to the lower-than-low feeling a reliever has when he walks off the mound after giving up a game-winning home run to the other team. That famous walk-off to Kirk Gibson was perhaps the lowest he's ever felt, although a close second was the ninth-inning home run he gave up to Roberto Alomar of the Blue Jays in Game 4 of the 1992 American League Championship Series. Alomar's two-run shot was not technically a walk-off because it only tied the game, but it capped a big comeback for the Jays, who went on to win in extra innings. They beat the A's for the pennant and ultimately won the World Series against the Braves.

The next year, the Blue Jays repeated as world champions when Joe Carter hit another famous walk-off in the sixth game of the World Series. That did not come off Eckersley, though. The victim was Phillies closer Mitch Williams, who could only hang his head in despair as the ebullient Carter bounded around the bases and fans at Toronto's SkyDome erupted.

In any case, only Eckersley, Williams, and other relievers truly know how lonely it is to walk off the field after giving up a game-winner: "It was a walk-off pitch," reliever Steve Howe said after a game in which he played the goat. "You throw the ball and walk off the mound."

In the summer of 2004, during his Hall of Fame induction speech, an emotional Dennis Eckersley talked about how his alcoholism had almost ruined his life. He spoke about the turning-point year of 1987, when, after being traded to the Athletics, he had to learn a new job on a new team while coming to accept the fact that he was an alcoholic, that he could not deny it anymore, and that his drinking was hurting himself and the people he loved.

"That off-season, after 1986, was probably the most difficult time in my life, both personally and professionally," he told the audience at Cooperstown, an audience that included many fellow members of the Hall of Fame, some of whom were moved to tears. "This is when my life changed forever. My career hit a major downturn and I was spiraling out of control personally. For the 12 years I pitched as a starter, I relied on raw talent and my ability to get through. It worked most of the time, but times were changing. No one knew then, but I was fighting a battle with alcoholism and I knew I had come to the crossroads of my life."

He concluded, "I'd like to leave an offering of a message of hope. That is, with the grace of God you can change your life, whoever you are."

Theo Epstein

It had come down to this: Yankees versus Red Sox in a one-game playoff to decide the winners of the American League East. The two teams had finished the 1978 regular season with identical records of 99 wins, 63 losses. The club that won one more game would go on to the League Championship Series, and the other would go home.

On the mound for the Yanks was their ace, left-hander Ron Guidry, finishing up a 25-win season that would have made Cy Young proud. But Guidry, although good, was not as good that day as journeyman right-hander Mike Torrez, who had pitched for New York the previous season but was in a Red Sox uniform now and carrying a 2 to 0 lead into the top of the seventh at Fenway with two men on and the dangerous Bucky Dent at the plate.

Dangerous? Not really. Not even close. Dent was a classic good-glove, no-hit shortstop; his batting average that year was a paltry .243. No home-run threat, he had hit only four dingers that season to date. Looking up from the batter's box at the 6-foot-5 Torrez, he fouled a pitch off his foot that brought the Yankees trainer hustling out from the dugout to examine him. Dent, walking off the sting, was declared fit to continue and the trainer scurried back to the dugout to watch a grand moment in recent Yankees history and an inglorious one for the Red Sox.

The delay may have bothered Torrez, because on the next pitch he gave up the home run that caused hearts to break across New England. Invariably described by writers as a "pop fly" over the Green Monster in left, Dent's improbable three-run pop gave the Yankees the lead in the game and carried them to a 5 to 4 win. They went on to handle the Royals in the League Championship Series and the Dodgers in the Series to repeat as world champions.

Theo Epstein was four years old at the time—"the Bucky Dent year," as he referred to it at his 2002 press conference announcing his appointment as the general manager of the Boston Red Sox. Growing up in Brookline, not far from Fenway, Theo says he was "a Red Sox fan from Day 1," which may not have been as early as four years old but probably wasn't long after. A bright kid from a talented family, he loved the Red Sox maybe as much as Humphrey Bogart loved Ingrid Bergman in *Casablanca,* the classic movie cowritten by Theo's granduncle and grandfather, Julius and Phillip Epstein.

Around the age of 12, Theo and his twin brother, Paul, were standing on the top of their living room couch in their house in Brookline, waiting, just waiting, for Boston reliever Bob Stanley to punch out Mookie Wilson on strikes so that they, and Red Sox fans everywhere, could celebrate the club's first world title since—well, since . . . *forever.*

Once again, it had come down to this: Boston versus New York, only this time the club from Gotham was the Mets and the setting was Shea Stadium. With two out in the tenth inning of the sixth game of the '86 Series, the American League champion Red Sox led the National League champion Mets 3 games to 2 and could close it out if Stanley could sneak one last strike past Wilson, who, irritatingly (at least to Red Sox fans like the Epstein brothers, poised on the top of their couches), kept fouling off pitch after pitch.

It can be reasonably argued that the Red Sox should have never gotten into this jam in the first place. With the game tied after regulation, Boston scored two runs in the top of the tenth to lead, 5 to 3, and then Red Sox reliever Calvin Schiraldi set down the first two Mets he faced in the bottom half of the inning. The Red Sox were one out from victory. But three consecutive Mets hits brought in a run, and Stanley emerged from the pen to replace Schiraldi.

Up came the switch-hitting Wilson, and choruses of "Moooo," the affectionate song sung by Mets fans whenever Mookie came to bat, cascaded around Shea. While trying in vain to get Mookie to swing and miss, or swing and hit a harmless grounder or fly to one of his fielders, Stanley let loose a wild pitch that let in another run. Some say Red Sox catcher Rich Gedman should have handled the ball. In any case, when the ball stopped rolling, the Mets' Kevin Mitchell had scored from third, tying the score at 5, and the Mets' Ray Knight, previously on first base, was standing ominously on second.

Probably at this point Theo and his brother climbed down from the couch and sat down. Or maybe they were too nervous to sit.

Stanley finally got the harmless ground ball he wanted, but it turned out to be not so harmless. In a grand moment in Mets history, and yet another inglorious one for the Red Sox, the grounder off Mookie's bat rolled through the legs of first baseman Bill Buckner. Ray Knight fled home and the ecstatic Mets won 6 to 5. Two days later, they took Game 7 and the world championship and extended a sorrowful string for the Red Sox. In each of its last four World Series—'46, '67, '75, '86—Boston has lost the seventh and deciding game.

Disappointed by their defeats but still faithful to them, Theo Epstein maintained his passion for the Red Sox—and baseball—while graduating with a degree in American Studies from Yale. After obtaining his law degree at the University of San Diego, he joined the San Diego Padres, eventually rising in the organization to become director of baseball operations. Earlier in his career he had found a mentor, Larry Lucchino, and when Lucchino became president and CEO of the Red Sox after the club was sold in 2002, the up-and-coming Epstein got called back to Boston to serve as assistant general manager. By November he was nobody's assistant, being named general manager of the Sox at age 28.

It was widely reported that Epstein was the youngest GM in baseball history, and although this may not be correct—some writers say Chub Feeney was only 25 when he started running the New York Giants after World War II—the boyish-looking Epstein is certainly no grizzled old-timer. Some have joked that when he grows up he can become a batboy.

His father, Leslie Epstein, a novelist and creative writing professor at Boston University, did not think his son was too young for the job, though.

"What's all the fuss?" he said. "At Theo's age, Alexander the Great was already general manager of the world."

Theo Epstein is one of a new wave of sharp young baseball general managers, some of whom—such as Paul Podesta of the Dodgers (Harvard) and Dan Dombrowski of the Tigers (Cornell)—are Ivy

League grads. With all this brainpower focused on the game these days, it has made some writers recall the quote by Sparky Anderson, who managed world championship teams in Cincinnati and Detroit. "I only have a high school education," said Sparky, "and I had to cheat to get that."

Eric Gagne

Born and raised in Montreal, Eric Gagne loved hockey as a boy, playing defenseman and throwing his big body around. Young Eric, who was always big for his age—he's now 6-2, 240 pounds—described himself as "a goon" whose job was to protect his more skilled teammates from opposing skaters who tried to get rough with them. If someone wanted to drop the gloves and fight, Gagne was always ready. He still has the scars on his hands from the fistfights he got into playing youth hockey in Canada.

Besides hockey, Gagne loved baseball, loved playing it, and loved going to see Expos games at Olympic Stadium. This was the sport he pursued professionally, although he struggled to find his groove as a pitcher in his early years in the game. After playing youth ball in Canada, he went to Seminole State Junior College in Oklahoma, where coach Lloyd Simmons liked what he saw in the burly, broad-shouldered, hard-throwing 19-year-old ex-goon with scars on his knuckles.

"He's an ornery guy," Simmons remembers, "but if a ballplayer doesn't have a little orneriness, you're wasting your time." Eric didn't just have a little orneriness, he had a whole bunch of it, and

Simmons encouraged him to really come after hitters and not back away from a challenge—traits that Gagne continues to exhibit to this day.

Eric grew up speaking French, the native language of Quebec, and he did not know much English when he arrived in Oklahoma. So he went on a crash course at Seminole State, taking English classes while watching MTV and other programs to learn the language.

After being signed by the Dodgers, Eric spent a few years bouncing around the minors. Some of his troubles on the mound had to do with the fact that he could not actually . . . *see*, which is something ballplayers generally need to do in order to succeed.

"At night I couldn't make out the catcher's signs," Gagne once said, describing his experience while pitching for San Antonio. "He'd ask for a curveball, and I'd throw a fastball off his chest. I said all right, that's enough, I need to see an eye doctor."

Valerie Hervieux, his then girlfriend, now wife, encouraged him in this regard, because when they were driving on the freeway at night and Eric was behind the wheel, he could not read the exit signs. He had to rely on her to tell him when to turn off.

But he could not use contacts, because in youth hockey an opposing player had accidentally high-sticked him in his left eye. Scar tissue had formed, and the contact would not sit in this eye the way it should. So the doctor prescribed glasses. In Eric's first game with glasses, he threw 17 straight balls without a strike because his sweat made the lenses fog up. Eventually, he settled on the prescription goggles that have become his trademark.

Initially, Gagne was a starter, but an ineffective one. Before his first start for the Dodgers, a team official asked him if he had a favorite song he wanted to have played as he entered the game. Nothing popped to mind, but Gagne had once seen a Guns N' Roses concert in Montreal and liked their music, so he thought of "Welcome to the

Jungle." Like his goggles, the Axl Rose anthem has become identified with him and it plays on Dodger Stadium loudspeakers every time he leaves the bullpen to come into a game.

"Being a starter, you have to be more mellow," Eric says. "It was boring. I'm not that kind of guy." The Dodgers eventually agreed with this assessment and tried him out as a reliever, where, among other duties, he served as an errand boy, supplying junk food—sunflower seeds, gum, Twinkies, candy bars, Cokes, Mountain Dews—to his teammates in the bullpen.

"It's not even the pitchers that eat all that stuff," Gagne laughs, looking back at those early days. "It's all for the bullpen catcher and coach. Pigs."

Another distinctive Gagne feature is his goatee, which former Dodgers teammate Paul Lo Duca refers to as his "Chia chin." Lo Duca is gone now (traded to the Marlins), but whenever the ninth inning rolled around and Los Angeles had a lead to protect, he'd say, "Bring on the goon," and everyone knew whom he was referring to. Other Dodgers affectionately call him the B.D.A.—Big Dumb Animal—which doesn't bother Gagne; he considers it a term of endearment.

When Eric and Valerie exchanged wedding vows, he said to her: "Valerie, I pledge you my heart and my arm." Which is not a vow to be dismissed lightly, considering what Gagne has done with that right arm: winning the 2003 Cy Young Award and setting an 84-game consecutive-save record.

True to his hockey roots and what Lloyd Simmons taught him, Gagne never backs down from a hitter, even if the hitter is Barry Bonds.

Many pitchers (and their managers) prefer to pitch away from Bonds in potentially game-deciding situations, but with the

Dodgers leading the Giants 3 to 0 in the ninth and no one on base, Gagne, then working on the 66th consecutive save in his string, decided to challenge the all-world San Francisco star head-on. Let the better man win.

Eric delivered a first-pitch fastball at 101 mph, according to the SBC Park scoreboard. Bonds fouled it off. Gagne's second pitch, also a fastball, came in at 100 mph, but Bonds did not miss this one, driving it deep into the center-field seats. Even so, the Dodgers escaped with the win and Gagne recorded the save.

After the game, Gagne was still buzzing about his confrontation with Bonds. "I loved it," he told a flock of reporters. "That was my best time in baseball. He is the best ever. There will never be anyone else like Barry Bonds."

Similarly charged up by his duel with one of the game's best closers, an admiring Bonds said, "When that ball hit my bat, that guy was just throwing straight cheddar."

Giants vs. Angels, Game 6, 2002 World Series

The Giants were coasting, 5 to 0, with one out in the top of the seventh at Edison Field in Anaheim. They led 3 games to 2 in the Series, which meant they were only eight outs away from winning the first world championship in San Francisco Giants history. Never had the Giants won a world title since moving from New York in 1958. And with right-hander Russ Ortiz twirling a one-hitter and seemingly in command of the pesky Angels, their first California championship appeared to be "as close to a mortal lock as there could be," in the words of sportswriter Tom Verducci, who was watching from the media seats.

So sure were the Giants of winning that some of their people had begun setting up the clubhouse for the postgame victory celebration, carting in 20 cases of champagne for the players to shake up and spray all over and douse one another's heads with and drink straight from the bottle. The specially made bottles featured the Giants logo with "World Champions" on the label.

Once the champagne was brought in, Giants aides started taking the bottles out of boxes and putting them in tubs of ice. The network television people were also doing their setups, designating a curtained area where the commissioner could award the team and individual honors (it was another mortal lock that Giants star Barry Bonds would be named Most Valuable Player), and where broadcasters could interview players and club representatives. The aides were taping plastic sheets over the openings of the players' lockers to protect what was inside. Plastic also covered the TV cameras to prevent them from being ruined by squirting champagne.

It was all set. The celebration was ready to begin. Then Troy Glaus and Brad Fullmer of the Angels delivered back-to-back singles, and Ortiz no longer appeared to have the command he did just moments before. Popping out of the dugout, Giants manager Dusty Baker, wearing wristbands just as he did in the '70s and '80s when he was a star outfielder for the Braves and Dodgers, showed no hesitation, tapping his right arm as he walked toward the mound. This was the signal that he intended to replace Ortiz and bring in right-handed reliever Felix Rodriguez, who was warming up in the bullpen.

When Dusty reached the mound, Ortiz handed over the ball, as pitchers inevitably do when their manager arrives to pull them from the game. Then the strangest thing happened. As Ortiz was starting to walk off, Dusty asked him whether he wanted to keep the ball as a souvenir.

★   ★   ★

Those not of a superstitious bent will say that what Dusty did mattered not at all. That the events that followed had more to do with failed pitching and timely hitting than anything else.

But superstitious people—and there are many in baseball who fit this description—would disagree. Against a team that had shown itself exceedingly capable of coming back against long odds (trailing 5 to 3 in the seventh inning of Game 5 of the American League Championship Series against the Twins, for example, the Angels scored *ten* runs), Baker had committed a grievous lapse of judgment. Giving your pitcher the game ball when the game wasn't over yet? Many longtime baseball observers could not recall a manager ever doing that, let alone doing it at such an important moment in the World Series.

It was Saturday night in Orange County. The southern California skies were cloudless and calm. No lightning bolts appeared in the sky, no booming peals of thunder (except, of course, the sound made by those inflatable sticks being slapped by Angels fans). But there are those who swear they felt something in the universe shift, somehow, when Ortiz, apparently surprised by Baker's offer, accepted his gift and walked off the mound with that ball in his glove. The baseball gods had been roused from their slumber, and they did not like what they saw.

Rested and ready, Felix Rodriguez had been a dependable reliever for the Giants all season, usually entering a game in the seventh to be followed in the eighth by Tim Worrell and finally, in the ninth, by closer Robb Nen. This was why Baker brought him in when he did. He and the two other Giants pitchers had been doing it all season long; all Dusty was asking of them was to do it for eight more outs.

The first batter Rodriguez faced was left-handed-hitting first baseman Scott Spiezio, whose father, Ed, was a former major league infielder. When Scott was a boy growing up in Illinois at the same time Dusty Baker was starring in the majors, he played lots of ball with his dad, who dreamed his son would grow up to be a big leaguer like him.

"When I was a kid playing in the backyard," recalled Scott, "my dad would make up situations—5–2, bottom of the ninth, bases loaded, two outs—and I'd be at the plate, pretending to be Don Mattingly or Mike Schmidt." But never in Scott's or Ed's fertile imaginations did they conceive of a situation quite like this: The Dominican-born Rodriguez throwing blazing stuff (up to 97 mph, according to the gun), and Scott fouling off four pitches and taking three more to run the count to 3 balls and 2 strikes.

Spiezio hit the next pitch into the right-field seats—"The ball was in the air long enough for me to say a prayer that it would go out," he said later—for a three-run homer.

A shaken Rodriguez survived the rest of the seventh with no more damage and gave way in the eighth to Worrell. The Giants were sticking to their script, which the Angels were rapidly rewriting. When Anaheim was trailing earlier in the game and seemingly out of it, Angels outfielder Darin Erstad kept repeating to his teammates in the dugout, "You never know. You never know."

Leading off the eighth, Erstad cracked a solo home run to bring the Angels to within one, and suddenly everyone in the Anaheim dugout (and possibly in the San Francisco dugout as well) seemed to know. When Tim Salmon and Garret Anderson followed with singles (Salmon going from first to third on Anderson's blooper to left, taking the extra base as the Angels did all series), Dusty Baker came out to the mound to yank Worrell. This time, when his reliever walked off, Dusty did not reward him with a game ball.

While all this was happening, Giants aides and TV people were scrambling around the visitors' clubhouse, pulling the champagne bottles out of the buckets of ice and putting them back into boxes and frantically pulling the plastic off the lockers. Meanwhile, the baseball gods continued to wreak havoc on the Giants.

In came Robb Nen, who threw a slider to Troy Glaus, who in turn bashed it for a double, scoring Salmon and Anderson and putting the Angels ahead, 6 to 5. The game ended with that score, and the Series was tied at three games apiece.

Afterward, outfielder Reggie Sanders of the Giants summed up the feelings of his teammates. "That was like a nightmare," he said. "It could have been over, but they fought back."

Sanders spoke solemnly in the funereal quiet of the Giants' clubhouse. Alongside their lockers were the strips of brown masking tape that the clubhouse people had not quite cleared off the walls before the game ended.

The next night, the Angels beat the Giants to win the first world championship in their franchise history. Troy Glaus was named MVP. In the off-season, Dusty Baker left San Francisco to become manager of the Chicago Cubs.

Lefty Gomez

One of the best (and funniest) pitchers in New York Yankees history was Lefty Gomez, whose birth name was Vernon Louis Gomez. Lefty never liked the name Vernon; he explained how he got it:

"When I was born, back in 1910, my Irish mother asked my Spanish father what I should be called. My father bent over the cradle, took one look at me, and then said to my mother, 'Let's call it quits.' Ma liked Vernon better."

★　★　★

Fast with a quip and a fastball, young Vernon Gomez grew up in the tiny California town of Rodeo, starting his minor league career with Salt Lake at age 17. The next year, he joined San Francisco in the Pacific Coast League, and despite his willingness to make jokes and have a little fun, he quickly earned a reputation for toughness on the mound. "He had plenty of guts, right from the start," said a sportswriter who watched him in those early days.

During a game, Nick Williams, the manager of the Seals (and a former scout who discovered Hall of Famer Paul Waner), would look down the bench at his pitchers and say, "Anyone got guts enough to challenge the enemy?"

Lefty would meet his gaze and say, "I'll challenge 'em." And invariably he did, winning 18 games for the Seals that season. The Yankees signed him and brought him up to the big club for the 1930 season. He was 21 years old.

Lefty Gomez made his big league pitching debut at Yankee Stadium on April 29, 1930, walking onto the field before the game to shake away his jitters and get a feel for the place. This was the "House That Ruth Built," a towering cathedral of baseball. His new teammates were storied figures such as Babe Ruth, Lou Gehrig, and Tony Lazzeri.

As if all that wasn't intimidating enough for a small-town kid of Hispanic and Irish descent, then there were all those *people* in the stands.

"I remember walking out just before that first game and looking around, and there were so many people in the stands that—well, there weren't just more people here than in my hometown but in my home *county*."

When the Yankees bought the contract of the 6-foot-2-inch Gomez from San Francisco, his listed weight was 175 pounds. But when he reported to the team, he weighed closer to 150. Looking at Gomez, a teammate said, "He was so thin that if he turned sideways to you, he would disappear from view."

Which led the Yankees to think that if they could get Gomez to add some bulk to his frame, he'd pitch more effectively. Lefty wasn't so sure: "Nobody can fatten up a greyhound," he said.

Nevertheless, longtime Yankees GM Ed Barrow kept after Gomez to gain some weight, citing the example of early-1900s New York right-hander Jack Chesbro, who had gotten hot as a pitcher after beefing up in the off-season. "If you'd only put on more weight," Barrow told Lefty, "you'll make the fans forget Chesbro."

So Lefty did. He gained some weight—and had a worse season than when he was skinny.

As Lefty put it, "Barrow told me that if I put on the 20 pounds, I'd make the fans forget Chesbro. Well, I put on the 20 pounds, and I damn near made them forget Lefty Gomez."

But the fans could not forget the hard-throwing, high-kicking left-hander, because he was too good. In 1931, his first full season in the bigs, he won 21 games. The next year, he topped that with 24 as the Yankees won the '32 Series. In 1933, he started the first-ever All-Star Game and, although he was an atrocious hitter, collected the first RBI in All-Star history with a single.

Asked what pitch he hit, Gomez replied, "With a bat in my hands, I couldn't tell a curve from a Cuban palm ball. I do recall that only one of my eyes was closed."

Gomez was as good at pitching as he was awful at hitting. (This was in the days when American League pitchers batted.) "They throw, I swing," he said about his hitting. "Every once in a while, they're throwing where I'm swinging and I get a hit."

Babe Ruth once bet him that he couldn't get 10 hits in a season. Lefty got a hit in his first game, then "went into a 42-game slump," as he said.

The following year, 1934, was the legendary All-Star Game in which the legendary Carl Hubbell struck out the legendary Babe

Ruth, Lou Gehrig, Jimmie Foxx, Al Simmons, and Joe Cronin all in a row. Lefty participated in that game too, although in a somewhat less legendary way.

After Bill Dickey broke up Hubbell's string of strikeouts with a single, Lefty came up to bat, although he wasn't sure why.

"You are looking at a lifetime .104 hitter," he said to Gabby Hartnett, the National League catcher. "Do you mind telling me what I am doing here?"

Hartnett had no answer. Lefty struck out.

Since Gomez was such a poor hitter, he didn't get on base very often. But one time he managed to scratch out a single and, after a hit by a teammate, advanced to third base. There, he asked third-base coach Art Fletcher if he could steal home.

"Listen," said Fletcher, "it's taken you years to get this far. And now you want to spoil it. The answer is no."

Lefty was the type of person often described as being "quick to laugh," with a wide grin and an upbeat personality. He once proposed the idea of a mechanically powered revolving goldfish bowl to make it easier for the fish to swim. Popular with fans, Lefty decided to take his comedy act to the vaudeville stage, only to quickly abandon it.

Asked why he so abruptly ended his foray into show business, he said, "I lasted three weeks, but the audiences didn't."

Despite Lefty's great success, some players hit him like they were batting off a tee. One of those was the powerful slugger Jimmie Foxx, who, joked Gomez, "had muscles in his hair."

One time, Foxx, muscles bulging, stood at the plate in a tight situation against Lefty, who kept shaking off the signs flashed to him by Yankees catcher Bill Dickey. Finally, an exasperated Dickey called time and trotted out to the mound to see what was wrong with his pitcher.

"What do you want to throw him?" he asked.

"Nothin'," said Lefty. "Maybe he'll just get tired of waiting and leave."

Part of Gomez's charm was that he never took himself too seriously. "The secret of my success," he always said, "was clean living and a fast outfield."

Beginning in 1936, when he joined the Yankees, a member of that fast New York outfield was Joe DiMaggio, who also became Lefty's roommate on the club.

"Joe ran down so many of my mistakes," Lefty was saying. "All I ever saw of Joe was the back of his uniform. I wouldn't have known what he looked like except that we roomed together."

Lefty pitched six World Series games in his career and won them all. But characteristically, after winning two games in the '36 Series by scores of 18 to 4 and 13 to 5, he joked, "I pitched two games and the Yankees could only get me 31 runs. See what I mean about pitching for the right club?"

Eventually, as it does with everyone, time caught up with Lefty. Late in his career, a writer asked him how hard he was throwing.

"I'm throwing hard as ever," he answered. "The ball's just not getting there as fast." Adding: "My manager spent ten years trying to teach me a change of pace. Now that's all I have."

After retiring as a pitcher, Lefty applied for a new job outside of baseball. The job application asked him the reason why he had left his last place of employment. "Couldn't get anybody out," Lefty wrote.

Lefty later got back into the game as a coach and minor league manager.

★   ★   ★

Fellow Hall of Famer Robin Roberts once said about Lefty, "I'd like to hear Lefty tell one story where he got someone out. I know he had a great record. He must have done something right sometime."

He certainly did, though you never heard it from Lefty. In 1969, after Neil Armstrong became the first man to walk on the moon, the American astronaut reportedly brought back to earth a mysterious white object that he could not identify.

"I knew immediately what it was," said Lefty. "It was a home-run ball hit off me by Jimmie Foxx."

Pedro Guerrero

In his prime, Pedro Guerrero was a heckuva ballplayer. A native of baseball-crazy San Pedro de Macoris in the Dominican Republic, he starred on the Dodgers' 1981 world championship team, sharing Most Valuable Player honors with two of his teammates in the World Series.

But Pedro occasionally had problems with reporters ("Sometimes they write what I say and not what I mean," he complained once) and even more problems in the field, as did his teammate on the Dodgers back then, Steve Sax.

Whereas Guerrero, an outfielder, mainly had trouble catching the ball when it was hit to him, Sax, a second baseman, had trouble throwing it. For reasons that were either physical or mental, or both, Sax often could not make the simple throw from second to first, bouncing it on the ground or tossing it too high or too wide.

One day, with Sax at second and Guerrero stationed behind him in right, Pedro had a perfectly horrible day in the field, dropping a few routine fly balls that led to a bunch of unearned runs, costing the Dodgers the game. Afterward, manager Tommy Lasorda took him aside and asked him what he was thinking about in the outfield.

"Two things," said Guerrero.

"Okay," said Lasorda. "What's the first thing?"

"God, don't let them hit the ball to me."

Appreciating his outfielder's honesty, Lasorda said, "All right. What's the other thing?"

"God, don't let them hit it to Sax."

When Pedro moved from Los Angeles to St. Louis in the late '80s, the Cardinals initially gave him a starting spot in the outfield. "Isn't that a mistake?" a reporter asked him.

"It's already a mistake if the ball's hit my way," he said with good humor.

Mostly, though, Guerrero played first base for the Cards, retiring in 1992 after 15 seasons in the majors. His lifetime batting average was .300.

Ozzie Guillen

When Ozzie Guillen was a fun-loving 17-year-old (he's still fun-loving, just older now), he was breaking into professional ball through the minor league system of the San Diego Padres. Back then, a scouting director for the Padres paid a visit to Ozzie's farm team to see how the young shortstop was doing.

Not so good, as it turned out. "I'm going to show you where I'm playing," Ozzie told the scouting director, leading him over to the dugout to the place on the bench where he usually sat during games.

"This is where I've been playing," he said, pointing to the bench, "this spot right there."

Ozzie wasn't being funny. He was serious. He didn't like sitting on the bench, he felt he should be starting, and he wanted the man to know it. The scouting director got the message, and after that Ozzie started to play more.

To their regret, the Padres gave up on Guillen too quickly, trading him to the Chicago White Sox, where he patrolled the middle infield for many seasons. Chicago's South Side team liked Ozzie not only because he was good (1985 American League Rookie of the Year, three-time All-Star) but because he was a likable fellow, always upbeat, a morale-booster in the clubhouse. He made friends easily, and most everyone on the club considered Ozzie his friend. When outfielder Ken Williams got traded from the Sox in the spring of 1989, Guillen happened to know about it before Williams did and it fell to Ozzie to be the one to tell his friend about it.

Ozzie showed up at Ken's house, and though Ken didn't believe the news at first, the tears in Ozzie's eyes told him, yes, it was true; he was no longer a White Sox, no longer Ozzie's teammate.

Fast-forward to late 2003. Ozzie had retired as a player after 13 seasons in Chicago and three more with three other clubs, and his old running mate Ken Williams had become general manager of the White Sox. Gone was the superserious Jerry Manuel as the club's skipper, and Williams was looking for his replacement. Somebody with a lighter touch than Manuel, perhaps, more of a player's manager, a person to loosen up the clubhouse atmosphere. What better man for the job, reasoned Williams, than Ozzie?

Never having managed in the big leagues, the 39-year-old

Guillen became manager of the Chicago White Sox, the first native Venezuelan to run a major league team.

"I want to have fun when I come to work," said Ozzie, "and I want my players to do the same." And so he did. One time, Ozzie decided his club needed to forget about a bad loss to the Twins as quickly as possible. After the game, he grabbed a boom box in the White Sox clubhouse, slipped in a salsa music CD, and turned the volume up, way up. Then he started dancing with a beat writer who covered the team for one of the Chicago papers.

"I've never seen that in my life," said White Sox catcher Sandy Alomar, Jr., who has seen a lot in his long career in the majors. But Ozzie's musicfest apparently did the trick. The next day, his players rebounded to drub the Twins.

In another game against their American League Central Division rivals, the Twins, Sox shortstop Jose Valentin was wearing a microphone for a television broadcast. The Sox were leading 4 to 2 in the eighth when Guillen trotted out from the dugout for a mound conference. Making the decision to replace his reliever, Ozzie gestured to the bullpen to send in closer Shingo Takatsu.

As they were waiting for Takatsu to come in, Ozzie explained to Valentin, "I'm changing pitchers just to be on TV, so my kids can see me in Florida." Valentin and the other infielders cracked up.

Guillen, a native Spanish speaker for whom English is a second language, often peppers his talk with colorful adjectives and adverbs—swearwords. He relies on a translator to converse with Takatsu, a native of Japan who does not speak English. Ozzie has made it clear to the translator that he wants Takatsu to be told everything he says. But one day Ozzie noticed that while he was talking in a team meeting, the translator wasn't saying anything.

Afterward, Ozzie confronted the translator. "Did you tell him everything I said?" he asked.

"No," answered the translator. "We don't have those words in Japanese."

Guillen has since learned several Japanese words. "The dirty ones," he explained.

People can misunderstand Ozzie even when he doesn't say a word. Two relievers were warming up in the Sox pen, righty Cliff Politte and lefty Damaso Marte, when Guillen decided to pull his starting pitcher from the game. Pointing to his right arm as he strode to the mound, Guillen meant to signal with his left because he wanted Marte, not Politte, to come in. But home-plate umpire Joe West insisted that Guillen honor his first choice, even if mistaken, and bring in the right-hander.

"Bring me whoever you want," the frustrated Guillen told West. But after Politte pitched well and the Sox won 3 to 0, Ozzie said, "Next time I go out there, I'm going to wave both arms."

Travis Hafner

Travis Hafner of the Cleveland Indians is a small-town guy with big-city power. He grew up in a North Dakota town with a population of 153. His high school graduating class had eight students in it—four boys, four girls. Jokes Travis, "The only thing easier than finishing in the top ten of my class was getting a date for the senior prom."

Now that he's become a big league slugger, Hafner can get as many dates as he likes. A big man (6-3, 240 pounds) with big hands and "legs as thick as pillars," in the words of sportswriter Tim Kurkjian, he hits, appropriately enough, big home runs. Another big thing about him is the size of his head. Noting this, his teammates started calling him "Shrek," a reference to the big-headed cartoon character.

Hafner doesn't like being called Shrek, though, so an ex-teammate came up with another nickname for him: Pronk, which is a combination of "project"—what Travis used to be before he blossomed as a major league hitter—and "donkey," what other players often call large, awkward guys like him.

Surprisingly perhaps, Travis doesn't mind Pronk, and certainly prefers it over Shrek. When a reporter told him he needed to find a new nickname besides Pronk because he was no longer a project, Hafner disagreed. "Without it," he explained, "I'm just Donk."

Home Runs

"A home run is a base hit that happens to leave the ballpark."

—Mark McGwire

A scrappy, pint-sized third baseman for the Tigers and other teams in the 1920s, Fred Haney almost never hit any base hits that happened to leave the ballpark. In 1923, he hit four; the year after that, one; the two years after that, zero. But in a game against the Yankees, he got lucky and boosted a pitch over the fence.

After the side was out, he was trotting out to take the field when he passed by Babe Ruth, who was jogging in from right. "Hey, Babe," Haney razzed him, "you're only 46 ahead of me now."

As the story goes, Babe hit a home run in his next at bat. As he was rounding the bases, he passed by Haney at third, saying, "How do we stand now, kid?"

A strong, muscular home-run hitter known as "The Beast," Jimmie Foxx "wasn't scouted," joked Lefty Gomez, "he was trapped." Gomez himself never had much luck against Foxx, who always seemed to hit him hard and far.

Once, after giving up a long home run to Foxx deep into the seats, Gomez was asked how far he thought the ball had traveled. "I don't know how far it went," he said, "but it takes 45 minutes to walk up there."

Foxx played first base for the Athletics when they called Philadelphia home, starring on back-to-back world championship teams in 1929 and '30. One of his World Series homers amazed all who saw it: "We watched it fly for two innings," said one wit.

In a career filled with long, long home runs, one of the longest of Mickey Mantle's career occurred during his 1951 rookie season on a spring training trip by the New York Yankees to southern California. There, while playing in an exhibition game at the campus of USC in Los Angeles, Mantle, a switch-hitter, hit a left-handed home run that soared over the center-field fence and beyond the width of a football field. Retired Yankees great Tommy Henrich and other observers estimated its flight at more than 600 feet.

"It was like a golf ball going into orbit," said USC baseball coach Rod Dedeaux, who also watched the ball fly and fly and fly. "It was hit so far it was like it wasn't real."

Two years later, Mantle hit another monster home run, this time in an American League game against the Washington Senators at Griffith Stadium in Washington, D.C. The ball traveled so far, it inspired Yankees public relations man Red Patterson to see if he could determine its actual distance. He left the press box area and found a boy in the bleachers who had seen the ball land. Using this as his guide, Patterson measured the distance as approximately 565 feet, thus giving birth to the term often used to describe such long blasts: "tape-measure home runs."

Despite playing the bulk of his home games in windy Candlestick Park, Willie Mays hit 660 home runs in his career, many of them tape-measure jobs. Just ask Warren Spahn, who, after giving up a homer to Mays, said, "It was a helluva pitch—for the first 60 feet."

This may have been the same homer that Lefty Gomez saw Mays hit off Spahn. "The ball came down in Utica," recalled Gomez. "I know. I was managing there at the time."

Willie Mays hit No. 600 off Padres pitcher Mike Corkins, who dejectedly returned to the San Diego dugout after giving up the blast.

"Why'd it have to be me, Skip?" he asked his manager, Preston Gomez.

"Son," replied Gomez sagely, "there've been 599 before you."

One year outfielder Alex Johnson hit eight home runs, the next year five, and a reporter asked him what he thought the difference was.

"Three," said Johnson matter-of-factly.

In Game 3 of the 1974 World Series, A's pitcher Catfish Hunter was coasting along with a 3 to 0 lead when first Bill Buckner in the eighth, and then Willie Crawford in the ninth, hit home runs for the Dodgers. The Athletics eked out a win, 3 to 2, and afterward reporters asked the North Carolina–born Hunter about the home runs.

"I had some friends here from North Carolina who'd never seen a homer before," he explained. "So I gave 'em a couple."

Reggie Jackson, who hit one of the longest All-Star Game home runs ever—in 1971, at Tiger Stadium; the ball was still rising when it hit the light tower above the second deck in right center field—loved to admire his big hits: "Every once in a while, if I really hit one, 450 feet or more, I'll say to myself, 'Damn that son of a gun's hit.' I've hit balls that wowed myself. 'Wow! *I hit that?*"

One of Reggie's home runs that wowed everyone who saw it, including Reggie, came at Fenway Park in Boston. "It was an insurance homer," he explained afterward. "That's why I hit it halfway to the Prudential Building." He added: "I hit that ball so far, my eyes weren't good enough to see it land. That one had some voltage."

In his rookie season with the Reds, outfielder Eric Davis hit two long opposite-field home runs in Cincinnati's Riverfront Stadium, one of them smashing against the upper-deck facade in right. After seeing this display of raw power by a young man only in his early twenties, Pete Rose, the Reds manager, took Eric aside to give him some advice.

"Don't you listen to nobody but me," Rose told him, "and you'll make a lot of money in this game."

One time in a game at the Big A in Anaheim, Athletics slugger Jose Canseco hit a hard line drive that the Angels shortstop, thinking he had a shot at the ball, jumped up to catch. But the ball flew over his head and kept rising and did not land until it banged against the empty seats beyond the left-center-field fence.

"Heck," said Dave Stewart, Jose's teammate on the A's, who was watching from the Oakland dugout, "the shortstop could have gotten on that thing and taken a flight to New York."

In another game at the Oakland Coliseum, Canseco hit a huge home run off Brewers reliever Paul Mirabella, who said afterward, "I wasn't worried about the ball going out of the park. I was just wondering if it was going to land in San Francisco. It had a crew of four on it and a meal."

Homer the Beagle

In 1962, the expansion New York Mets took the field for the first time, becoming one of two new clubs (the other was the Houston Colt 45s, now Astros) to join the National League. To say the Mets were not very good is an understatement of the most extreme kind. They were, in fact, horrendous, losing 120 games that first season and setting a record for futility, as the sportswriters like to say.

The leader of this ragtag band of ne'er-do-wells was Casey Stengel, who, two years earlier, had been fired as manager of the New York Yankees following their loss to the Pirates in the 1960 World Series. In his 12 years with the Yankees, Stengel had led them to ten American League pennants and seven world championships, including five in a row from 1949 to 1953. Nevertheless, the Yankee front office judged Stengel to be too old to manage anymore, which drew this famous response from Casey: "I'll never make the mistake of being 70 again."

The Mets hired Casey as much for his managing skills as the fact that he remained highly popular in New York, a colorful, much-beloved character with a sharp, genuine wit and an appreciation for the absurdity of the situation he now found himself in. Born in the last decade of the nineteenth century, the Ol' Perfesser had been around the game seemingly forever, but he had never seen anything to compare to the glorious awfulness that was the '62 Mets.

Those Mets (and the '63 team as well, which lost 111 games, not quite as bad as the previous year, though still pretty bad) consisted of as colorful a band of losers as have ever been assembled on a ballfield.

The '62 club obtained its players through an expansion draft, choosing men that the other National League teams did not want and so left unprotected. Among these were aging veterans such as first baseman Gil Hodges and infielder Don Zimmer, whose talents had eroded with time. Then there was a whole roster full of players who did not have that much talent to begin with. "Look at that guy," Stengel told sportswriters during spring training, pointing to a Mets player. "He can't hit, he can't run, and he can't throw. Of course, that's why they gave him to us."

For their first selection in the expansion draft, the Mets chose a catcher because, as Casey rightly stated, "You have to have a catcher, because if you don't, you're likely to have a lot of passed balls."

One of the catchers on the Mets (not the first one picked) was Chris Cannizzaro, a 24-year-old cast-off from the Cardinals who was brought to New York for his skills behind the plate. "Canzoneri," said Stengel—butchering the pronunciation of Chris's name, as he did with the names of so many of his players, particularly those with more than one syllable—"Canzoneri is the only defensive catcher who can't catch."

Another catcher on the Mets was Clarence "Choo Choo" Coleman, who was once asked by a radio interviewer what his wife's name was and what was she like. "Her name is Mrs. Coleman," said Choo Choo, "and she likes me."

The most famous, and famously bad, player of these Mets was error-prone first baseman Marv Throneberry, referred to by Casey as "Thornberry." Known as "Marvelous Marv," because he was not, Throneberry, or Thornberry if you like, earned his lasting reputation in the game from his klutzy play in the field and his even klutzier baserunning. One time he blasted a two-run triple but the umpire called him out for failing to touch first base, which caused his manager to rush from the Mets' dugout to protest the decision.

Mets first-base coach Cookie Lavagetto, however, intercepted Casey before he could utter a syllable. "It won't do any good, Casey," Cookie told him. "He missed second base, too."

Gazing down the dugout at Marvelous Marv and Choo Choo and Chris Canzoneri and others like them was what compelled Casey to utter his immortal line: "Can't anybody here play this game?" The answer, for the most part, was no, and Mets management continually brought in new players, while releasing or trading others, in an effort to improve its fortunes on the field. (Marvelous Marv himself came over in a trade.) But nothing much worked, and at one point in the '62 season the club lost 17 straight games.

"The losing doesn't bother me," Casey, the aging philosopher, said. "It's the not winning that hurts." The not winning also affected Rheingold beer, which was then a TV and radio sponsor of the Mets. And, looking for ways to spice up the broadcast coverage of yet another predictable Met loss, Rheingold's advertising agency came up with an idea: Homer the Beagle.

The call went out to Hollywood and Rudd Weatherwax, who was the trainer of Lassie, a collie (actually there were a number of Lassies, not just one) who starred in movies and a popular TV show of the era. Besides Lassie, the Weatherwax family had trained dogs for *Old Yeller*, and Toto of *The Wizard of Oz*. Equipped with the necessary pedigree and training, Homer set forth on an odyssey to the ancient Polo Grounds of New York, where the Mets played for their first couple of years until moving to Shea.

Homer's job was to entertain the fans by running around the bases and sliding into home plate after each Mets home run. The squat little black-and-white hound with the sad, brown eyes and floppy ears was ready to do his duty, performing admirably during practice, but Casey Stengel, who hated the dog, would not let him sit in the dugout with the team as originally planned. Also complicating matters was the fact that the Mets did not hit many home runs in those days and Homer never got much of a chance to perform his stunt.

Finally, the big day arrived. Someone on the Mets actually hit a home run, and after he had rounded the bases and touched home plate, it was Homer's turn to do the same. His handler let him go. Off he went, touching first *and* second (unlike Marv Throneberry), but with all the noise in the stadium he got confused and started running crazily around the outfield. It took six people, including his handler and three players in the field, to catch poor Homer. The Mets figured they'd seen enough and decided that although things were bad, perhaps they weren't as bad as all that, and they returned him to Hollywood.

Fred Hutchinson

First as a pitcher, then as a manager, Fred Hutchinson was as hardnosed as they came. They called him the Big Bear, because he could get as angry as one. Another nickname for him was Stone Face, because, as sportswriter Leonard Koppett remarked, he "always looked like his team had just hit into a game-ending triple play."

Didn't matter if his club was up by ten runs or down by ten, Hutch always looked the same during a game: glum. Joe Garagiola cracked that he was actually happy inside, it's just that his face didn't know it.

Fred Hutchinson's toughness derived in part from his father, a prominent Seattle physician, who opposed an increase in trolley fares in the city when Fred was a boy growing up in the 1920s and

'30s. Dr. Hutchinson rallied the public against the increase, which he criticized as exorbitant and unfair. Nevertheless, despite his opposition, the fare increase went into effect, raising the price from a nickel to a dime.

One evening after seeing patients all day, Dr. Hutchinson decided to ride the trolley home. But when he boarded the train and tried to pay with a nickel, the driver informed him that the fare was no longer five cents and that if he wanted to ride, he needed to pay a dime.

"You mean to say if I don't pay more I will have to get off and walk home?" asked Dr. Hutchinson.

The driver nodded yes.

The stubborn Dr. Hutchinson then proceeded to do exactly that, walking home on the trolley tracks, right in front of the trolley car, the train following behind him at the doctor's walking pace. Only after Dr. Hutchinson reached home and stepped off the tracks could the trolley resume its normal speed.

Fred's brother Bill-became a doctor like their father, but Fred chose a different career path: delivering hard medicine to batters as a pitcher. After graduating from Seattle's Franklin High, Fred rapidly made the jump into pro ball, joining the hometown Rainiers of the Pacific Coast League. In 1938, his first and only year with the club, he won 25 games and the *Sporting News* selected him Minor League Player of the Year for the country.

But even as a teenager Fred began to develop a reputation as a fellow with a nasty temper.

If one of his teammates in the field made an error behind him, he'd yell at him, throw his glove on the ground, and stomp around the mound. In the dugout and locker room after a loss, he'd throw bats, toss chairs, kick over the water cooler. And if Fred lost a game when the club was on the road, well, watch out. He'd go back to his hotel room and trash the joint: punching things, throwing things, kicking over anything that wasn't bolted down.

Finally, his roomie on the road, an outfielder named Edo Vanni, had to tell him to knock it off because Hutch had wrecked his bed and Edo didn't have a place to sleep. He had to spend the night on the floor.

When, at age 19, Hutchinson signed a contract with the Detroit Tigers, he and his mom posed for a wire-service photo in the kitchen of their Seattle home. With her graying hair pulled back in a bun, Nona Hutchinson wore horn-rim glasses and an apron as she poured a glass of milk for her son from a bottle. Fred, his broad face smiling and wearing none of the anger that it so often did on a ballfield, was turned toward his mom, whose free hand rested on his shoulder. A bowl of cereal was on the table in front of him as if he were about to eat breakfast, although he was dressed in a coat and tie, which probably wasn't his normal breakfast garb.

Like any young prospect setting off for the big leagues for the first time, Hutchinson left home full of optimism. Things did not quite work out for him right away in Detroit, and as with many others of his generation, his playing career came to a stop with the advent of World War II. But after the war he became a reliable pitcher for the Tigers, winning 18 games in 1947 and posting solid marks while becoming known as a tough battler.

Then, in the early 1950s, with his career as a pitcher winding down, the Tigers surprised baseball by naming him as their manager. What was so surprising about the choice was his relatively young age—33—and the fact that he had not coached or managed one day in the big leagues. Additionally, most managers tend to be former position players, not pitchers. But anyone who had ever dealt with Dr. Hutchinson's son knew he could handle the job.

Hutch was born to be a manager. It suited his temperament. He liked being in charge, and could accept responsibility for the decisions he made.

"For five innings," he said once, "it's the pitcher's game. After that, it's mine."

Hutch took his job seriously, and as always, he took losing seriously too. He couldn't stand it. After a bad loss, he'd get mad and start throwing things, although, as a sportswriter once wisely pointed out, "Hutch doesn't throw furniture. He throws rooms."

On the road, the Yankees would sometimes follow the Tigers into a city to play the team that Detroit had just faced. Yankees catcher Yogi Berra always knew whether Hutch's Tigers had won or lost their games by the condition of the visitors' clubhouse when he arrived.

"If we got stools in the clubhouse, I knew he'd won," said Yogi. "Otherwise, we got kindling."

Nobody liked to mess with Hutch on a tear, including umpires. "I tangled once with Fred and the goddamn veins in his neck got so big I wanted to run," recalls umpire Cece Carlucci. "It seemed that all the blood ran to his face. He looked in my face, and it seemed like his neck got bigger."

When he was in St. Louis, Hutch managed former Whiz Kid Del Ennis on the Cardinals. After Ennis made an out with the bases loaded, Hutch got so furious that he grabbed Del's bat and smashed it against the dugout steps, banging it repeatedly against the concrete. When he could not break the bat, only dent it, he gave it back to Ennis.

"Keep it," he told him. "It's got good wood."

A friend once said that in a wrestling match between Hutch and a bear, he'd bet on Hutch. Old Stoneface could get players to bend to his will just by casting a cold stare in their direction, not uttering a word. But when he did speak his mind, said an admirer, Mickey Mantle, "he didn't sneak around corners to do it."

One time Moe Drabowsky was pitching with the bases loaded but had run the count to three balls on the hitter at the plate. One more ball and he'd walk in a run.

Hutch walked to the mound to talk to his pitcher. He was not pleased.

"Look around you, Moe," he said. "The bases are full. Where the [bleep] you gonna put this guy?"

Hutchinson's greatest success as a manager came in 1961, when he led the Cincinnati Reds to the National League pennant. But two years later, around Christmastime, his physicians delivered a shocker. He had cancer, they told him.

"One day you're fine," he said upon learning the news, "and the next day you have cancer."

He returned home to Seattle, but his brother, a physician, sadly confirmed the diagnosis.

In failing health, Hutch returned to manage the Reds for the '64 season. Growing weaker and sicker as the summer wore on, he stayed on the job till August, when his illness forced him to step aside. But he did not react with his customary anger. He was calm and controlled, and the grace in which he handled himself during this hard time earned him admirers in and out of baseball. As tough as he was, he had met a tougher opponent, and Hutch knew it.

A month after the regular season ended, Fred Hutchinson was dead. He was 45 years old. The Reds later retired his jersey, No. 1, the first number ever retired by the club in its long history.

Ichiro

The moment Ichiro "arrived" as a major league ballplayer occurred early in his 2001 rookie season. It came in a game between his Seattle Mariners and their rivals in the American League West, the Oakland Athletics. Terrence Long, then with the Athletics, was on first base. An A's batter laced a single to right and Long took off running, rounding second and heading for third in a direct challenge to the throwing arm of Ichiro, who was playing right field.

At the time, Ichiro—like Pele or Shaq, only one name is needed to identify him—was unknown to his fellow major leaguers (and most Americans), many of whom doubted his chances of making it here. Sure, he had won the Japanese professional batting crown seven times and set a slew of records there. Sure, the Mariners had paid $13 million to his former club, the Orix Blue Wave, to obtain his rights, signing him to a $14 million contract over three years. But Ichiro was small and skinny (5-9, 160 pounds) by major league standards, and while Japanese and Asian pitchers were doing well in the big leagues, no Japanese national had ever been a regular position player in either the American or National League.

So Terrence Long, who was not a Maserati on the base paths but who was not a truck either, was going to find out what kind of arm the 27-year-old rookie had. He found out, all right. The ball flew on a line and arrived in the third baseman's glove just as he was sliding into the bag. "It was going to take a perfect throw to get me," Long said afterward, "and it was a perfect throw."

Fans in Seattle refer to that play as "The Throw." And sportswriters pulled out their most colorful language to describe it:

"It was like Ichiro threw a coin to third base . . . like out of a cannon, quick and powerful . . . He threw a laser . . . It was like something out of *Star Wars.*"

The man who unleashed The Throw was more matter-of-fact. Speaking through a translator, he said, "The ball was hit right to me. Why did he run when I was going to throw him out?"

That appears to be the Ichiro style: Do the deed on the field and let others do the talking: "I learned a long time ago, whether I have a very good day or a very bad day, I never say it. You're better off letting others do it." In 2001, of course, Ichiro had many more good days than bad, although it took more than The Throw to convince some of his early critics.

In a game in Oakland, fans in the right-field stands yelled racial slurs and threw coins and other objects at him. One man hit him in the head with a quarter. When Ichiro stared coldly back at him from the field, the man mocked him by taking a Japanese-like bow.

In talking about the incident after the game, Ichiro spoke through his translator, who said, "Something came out of the stands and hit me."

When he heard this, in English, Ichiro corrected his translator and had him say instead: "I must correct my previous interpretation. Something came out of the sky and hit me."

Asked what exactly that something was, Ichiro said, "I couldn't tell if it was rain or money coming down."

The reporters quizzing Ichiro may have begun to sense that he was using humor to shift attention away from the incident. They then asked him if anything like this had ever happened to him in Japan.

"Of course it happened there," he replied. "Anytime you come in as a visiting team, things fall out of the sky. The gods once threw an aluminum can at me."

After seeing Ichiro play and realizing that he was indeed the real deal, baseball fans in this country elected him to the 2001 All-Star team with 3.4 million votes, the most votes of any player and the most ever for a rookie. Americans came to know his story: how his father, Nobuyuki Suzuki, had taught him the game when he was a youngster; how he had signed with the Blue Wave out of high school; how he won his first batting title in Japan (.385) in '94, his first full season in pro ball; how he had once gone 216 consecutive at bats without striking out; how he had earned a flawless 1.000 fielding percentage one season; and more.

American sportswriters, eager to fill in the details on the Ichiro phenomenon, questioned him closely on some of his habits that seemed strange to U.S. baseball fans. Before each game, Ichiro rubs a small wooden stick along the sides and bottoms of his feet in order to stimulate blood circulation and promote energy and vitality. Observing this practice, a reporter asked Ichiro what he called the stick.

"Wood," he said.

Ichiro is not one to glamorize what he does. "Baseball is just baseball," he says. Nevertheless, lots of people glamorize *him*. His is the single most recognized face in Japan. If you sent a letter to that country and simply wrote "Ichiro" on the envelope without an address, most everyone in Japan would know whom you were talking about and the letter might get to him. A Japanese magazine reportedly offered to pay $1 million to any photographer who snapped a picture of him in the buff.

Especially during his groundbreaking 2001 season, throngs of Japanese media followed him wherever he went. One morning in Seattle, he supposedly opened his garage door to go to Safeco Field—and two Japanese TV crews were already waiting for him in the driveway. The cameras rolled as he calmly backed his car out and headed off to the park.

Playing in right at Safeco, Ichiro took off running as a fly ball soared over his head toward the fence. The ball appeared headed out of the park until he leaped up above the top rail of the fence and snatched it out of the air. His momentum carrying him forward, his body hit the ground and he rolled forward in a gymnastic-style somersault. Popping up to his feet, he showed the ball in his glove to the umps. Then, coolly adjusting his sunglasses, made slightly crooked by the tumble, he rifled the ball back in to an infielder as the hometown fans let out a mighty roar.

Asked later how he had managed such a feat, he shrugged. "It was a fly ball. I caught it."

Another game, this time against the Orioles, and another spectacular catch. Actually, two of them. "The catch he made on [Brady] Anderson's ball down the line and the catch he made on [Jerry] Hairston's ball—no other right fielder in the American League makes those plays," said an admiring Mike Hargrove, the Orioles manager.

Ichiro himself was not sure which catch was the harder of the two. "It's tough to say which one was the toughest, because each fly ball had a different characteristic," he said.

In April 2001, Rob Dibble, the former Nasty Boy reliever turned ESPN commentator, mocked Ichiro's ability to perform in the American major leagues. He said on the air that he'd run around Times Square naked if the Japanese star won the batting title in the United States. Furthermore, he'd tattoo 51, Ichiro's jersey number, on his butt if Ichiro won the title. If Ichiro even hit .300 or better, Dibble added, he'd run around Times Square wearing only a Speedo swimsuit.

In 2001, Ichiro won the American League batting title with 242 hits and a .350 average, stole a league-leading 56 bases, and won both Rookie of the Year and Most Valuable Player honors. After the season ended, Dibble issued an apology to Ichiro, calling his previous comments "a lame attempt at wit and humor." He apparently did not run around Times Square naked, as promised, nor was 51 tattooed on his rear.

Reggie Jackson

"The only reason I don't like playing in the
World Series is I can't watch myself play."

—Reggie Jackson

One of the greatest home-run hitters of all time and one of the
greatest talkers of all time is Reginald Martinez Jackson, who starred
on one of the greatest teams of all time, the Oakland Athletics of the
early 1970s. The A's won three consecutive World Series titles from
1972 to 1974. On a team of stars, Reggie stood out for his good
looks, his powerful physique, his impressive throwing arm and his
even more impressive home-run power, his ability to produce lively
copy for the media, his showmanship, his joy in being center stage.

"There was only one big home-run guy, one big hero," said Dave
Duncan, a teammate of Reggie's in Oakland, who's now a pitching
coach for the Cardinals. "That was Reggie. He was born to the job."

Another of his teammates on the A's, Darold Knowles, assessed
Reggie slightly differently: "There isn't enough mustard in the
whole world to cover this hot dog."

After leaving Oakland in 1975, the big dog played a year with the
Orioles before becoming a free agent able to sign with any club with
enough dough to afford him. One of his most zealous suitors was
George Steinbrenner, owner of the New York Yankees.

Although the Yankees had won the 1976 American League pennant, the Reds had swept them in the World Series, and Steinbrenner badly wanted Jackson's potent left-handed bat in the New York
lineup.

"What do you want more than anything in the world?" he asked Reggie in a phone conversation after the end of that season.

Reggie thought about it a minute before replying, "A Corniche Rolls Royce," which at the time sold for more than $60,000.

"Done," said George. "All I'm asking in return is the right to be the last person to talk to you before you make up your mind."

Reggie agreed and took ownership of a new Rolls, compliments of George. After more wooing by the persistent Yankees boss—"It was like trying to hustle a girl at a bar," Steinbrenner said later— Reggie put his signature to a five-year contract with the Yankees for the then-colossal sum of nearly $3 million.

If there ever was a perfect marriage between a ballplayer and a city, it was Jackson and New York.

At the press conference held at the Americana Hotel in Manhattan to announce his signing, the newest Yankee wore a gray flannel Geoffrey Beene suit with a blue tie and a gold bracelet on his wrist that spelled out "Reggie" in diamonds. On one of his fingers, impossible to miss, was one of the three gaudy world championship rings he had earned in Oakland.

"I didn't come to New York to become a star," he told the room packed with reporters and cameras. "I brought my star with me."

The Reggie Jackson Era in New York had begun.

The following year, Reggie showed up for Yankee spring training camp and, as always, started saying memorable things to reporters:

"You never met anyone like me. I'm not just a ballplayer. I'm a multifaceted person, a myriad of personalities. I'm a businessman who happens to be an athlete."

"I haven't come here to create controversy. I don't know me that way. That's not the me I read about. The only publicity I want is to be at the top of the home-run and RBI leaders every day."

"Part of the reason they pay me is that . . . I'm the hunted. I'm the hunted on the team of the hunted."

One of Reggie's teammates on the Yankees, Catfish Hunter, had also played with him in Oakland, so he knew his bombastic personality well. "The thing about Reggie is that you know he's going to produce," said Catfish. "And if he doesn't, he's going to talk enough to make people think he's going to produce."

The North Carolina–born Hunter, who was also pretty good with a quote, delivered one of the best lines on Jackson: "Reggie's a really good guy, he really is. He'd give you the shirt off his back. Of course, he'd call a press conference to announce it."

When Reggie was in Oakland, he said, "If I was playing in New York, they'd name a candy bar after me." Early in his first season in New York, Standard Brands company announced it would soon go into production on a new "Reggie!" candy bar.

Reggie's most controversial moment as a Yankee—well, actually, there were a whole slew of them, but this was one of the biggest— came later in the year with the publication of the June issue of *Sport* magazine.

"You know this team," Reggie was quoted as saying. "It all flows from me. I'm the straw that stirs the drink. It all comes back to me. Maybe I should say me and Munson, but really, he doesn't enter into it."

Munson was Thurman Munson, the popular Yankees captain and team leader who had won MVP honors in 1976. But with Reggie now on the scene, fan and media attention had shifted away from the far less glamorous, far less quotable catcher who, said Reggie, was "being so damned insecure" about Jackson's arrival on the team.

Reggie continued, "Munson can't intimidate me. Nobody can. You can't psyche me. You take me one-on-one in the pit and I'll whip you."

And: "Munson thinks he can be the straw that stirs the drink, but he can only stir it bad."

And: "If I wanted to, I could snap him [Munson]. Just wait until I get hot and hit a few out, and the reporters start coming around and I have New York eating out of the palm of my hand . . . he won't be able to stand it."

And: "Don't you see there is no way I can play second fiddle to anybody? That's just not in the cards. There ain't no way."

Asked for a response to these remarks, Munson angrily replied, "He's a [bleeping] liar. How's that for a quote?"

Adding to the sting was the fact that Reggie's big new contract was paying him far more than what Munson was getting. "I'm just happy to be here," Thurman added sarcastically. "I wish George would buy me a Rolls-Royce."

Asked once what he'd do if problems cropped up on the Yankees, Reggie said, "I can deal with it like a big dog."

Well, many problems did indeed crop up with the Yankees that year—between Jackson and Steinbrenner, Jackson and manager Billy Martin, Jackson and Munson and other teammates. One of the teammates who clashed with Reggie was Mickey Rivers, an eccentric but also highly quotable Yankee, who told him one day, "Look at you, man. You got a white man's first name, a Spanish man's second name, and a black man's third name. No wonder you're all screwed up. You don't know who the hell you are."

After arguing one day with Rivers and getting nowhere, Reggie said, "I can't believe I'm arguing with a guy who can't read or write."

To which Mickey hotly responded, "You better stop reading and writing, Reggie, and start hitting."

Eventually Reggie, Mickey, Thurman, and the rest of the squabbling Yankees started hitting, Catfish and the staff started pitching, and New York repeated as American League champions, advancing to the World Series against the Dodgers. In the sixth and final game of that Series, Reggie launched three home runs into the night to lead the Yankees to the world title, and as he had predicted, all of New York was eating out of his hand.

"I never thought of myself as the equal of Ruth and Gehrig and Yankees like that," he said in an uncharacteristically modest moment after his epic evening, "but for one night I was."

The following season, a reporter asked Jackson what he had thought about during a five-game period in which he was suspended from the Yankees for rebelling against Billy Martin.

Reggie pondered the question a long time before answering. "The magnitude of me," he said somberly.

For this and many other remarks, veteran *New York Times* sportswriter Dave Anderson named Jackson the second-most-quotable athlete of all time, ranked behind only one other straw that could really stir the drink, Muhammad Ali.

Derek Jeter

Derek Jeter first announced he was going to play for the New York Yankees when he was eight years old. It was late in the evening at his home in Kalamazoo, Michigan. He was in his pajamas. So were his mom and dad. After making his announcement, young Derek went to bed.

On eighth-grade graduation day at St. Augustine's Elementary School in Kalamazoo, Derek and a bunch of his friends decided to make up stories about what they'd be doing if they all came back together for a reunion in ten years. Each of them wrote his or her story in the St. Augustine's yearbook.

The story penned by 13-year-old Derek proved prescient: "Derek Jeter, a professional ballplayer for the Yankees, is coming around. You've seen him in grocery stores and on Wheaties boxes, of course."

As a youngster, Derek weighed about 70 pounds, as he recalls, "with two rolls of quarters in my pockets." He played in the Westwood Little League in Kalamazoo and had a poster of Dave Winfield on his bedroom wall. Winfield was his favorite Yankee. Derek's parents knew their son was in his room because they could hear him tossing a tennis ball against the wall, playing catch with himself.

Derek loved to play catch. He'd play it all the time with anyone who'd play with him, including his grandmother, Dorothy Connors. In the summers, Derek and his sister would visit their grandma and grandpa, who lived in New Jersey, where Derek was born and spent his infant years.

Grandma Dorothy was a huge ball fan, just huge. And she loved the Yankee, too. When Babe Ruth died in 1948 and his body lay in state at Yankee Stadium, she was one of the 100,000 people who stood in line to pass by his casket and pay her respects. She and Derek would eat crackers and listen to Yankees games on the radio or watch them on TV. It was Grandma Dorothy who took Derek to the Bronx to his first game at Yankee Stadium, and she was one of the people who'd get up early with him to play catch.

Derek was an early riser, as was his grandmother, and the two of them would sometimes go out to the backyard as early as 6 A.M. Though she was older he didn't ease up on her, throwing the ball so hard her palm would hurt although she had a glove on. The ball would sting, but she'd catch it and throw it back, and they'd play until it was time to go inside and have breakfast.

Two men were sitting in the stands watching Jeter at a baseball camp during his sophomore season at Kalamazoo Central High. One of them was veteran Yankees scout Dick Groch. The other was a college coach. Both were impressed by the speed, throwing arm, hitting ability, and overall smarts of the teen shortstop.

That kid is going to be a heckuva college player when he graduates, said the college coach. He added that as soon as camp was over, he was going to begin recruiting him and write him a letter.

Groch looked at him. "Save your stamp," he told him bluntly. "You're looking at something special."

What Groch meant by this was that the Yankees were not going to let a prospect as talented as Derek Jeter slip by them. Over the next two years, he and eight other Yankees scouts tracked Jeter wherever he played. In his senior season at Kalamazoo Central, he won High School Player of the Year for the United States. The Yankees chose him with their first pick in the amateur draft, signing him for $800,000. He never played an inning of college ball.

What the scouts liked about Jeter, besides his skills and intelligence, was his exuberance for the game. The kid just loved to play. Dorothy Connors called her grandson "excitable." Groch put it another way: "He's like a kid at a family picnic." On his scouting report for the Yankees, Groch gave him a rating of 64, which indicated the makings of an above-average major leaguer. More telling were his comments in another part of the report:

"Major league shortstop," he wrote. "Blue chip. A Yankee."

In the spring of '96, the Yankees had a decision to make: whether to start Tony Fernandez or Jeter at shortstop. The 21-year-old Jeter was clearly a rising star in the organization, having jumped three rungs up the baseball ladder—from Class A Tampa to Double A Albany to Triple A Columbus—in one year and been named Minor League Player of the Year in 1994.

But Fernandez, a dozen years older than his rival, had won Gold Gloves and played on All-Star teams, and everyone on the Yankees knew how much The Boss, George Steinbrenner, liked veterans for their experience and disliked rookies for their lack of same. So even though Yankees manager Joe Torre had practically awarded the job to the fresh kid from Kalamazoo, it was hardly a done deal that Jeter would start.

Then in late March, a week or so before Opening Day, the unlucky Fernandez broke his elbow in practice. The injury kept him out of the lineup the entire season, and he eventually left the team. Jeter became the Opening Day starter for the Yankees and seized the opportunity, hitting a home run in his first at bat and making a running catch of a bloop fly in short left field that helped preserve New York's lead and win the game. He stayed the regular shortstop, batted .314, and won the Rookie of the Year Award.

Only the greatest of Yankees receive jerseys with single numerals. Babe Ruth wore 3, Lou Gehrig 4, Joe DiMaggio 5, Mickey Mantle 7, Yogi Berra 8. The club has retired all these numbers and they cannot be worn by other players. Billy Martin, who had a love-hate relationship with owner George Steinbrenner but who loved the Yankees with a passion, wore 1 when he managed the club. In 1961, Roger Maris broke Babe Ruth's single-season home-run record with 61 home runs. His jersey number was 9. One indication of the high hopes the Yankees had for Jeter was the number they gave him: 2.

The Yanks won the title when Jeter was a rookie, and after the World Series, New York City held a parade for the team in the Canyon of Heroes in lower Manhattan. He and teammate Jim Leyritz rode the subway to the parade, which, as Jeter remembers, "started on the train. The train was packed with so many fans, I wasn't sure if we were going to get off."

Three million people attended that parade, more than a few of the women holding up signs that read, "Marry Me, Derek" and

"No. 2, Be My No. 1," which was not a new phenomenon. As soon as Jeter joined the team, the handsome, dark-haired, olive-skinned son of biracial parents caught the attention of female fans.

"We go from town to town and there are girls crying and screaming for him," said a teammate. One of those Yankee immortals, Yogi Berra, couldn't figure how Jeter managed to handle all the attention: "I was only 22 when I came up, but I didn't have to go through what he goes through. I didn't have all those girls screaming at me. I wasn't as good-looking as him."

The Yankees slipped in 1997, then won everything three years in a row: 1998, 1999, 2000. But in the 2001 postseason, going for their fourth straight championship, they dug a big hole for themselves, losing the opening two games of the American League Division Series to the Oakland Athletics at Yankee Stadium.

In Game 3 of that series, having switched coasts to the Oakland Coliseum, New York led 1 to 0 in the bottom of the seventh when A's outfielder Terrence Long stung a Mike Mussina pitch into the right-field corner. With two outs in the inning, Jeremy Giambi, who was on first base, was moving as fast as his legs would carry him, rounding second and third and headed for home, hoping to score the tying run.

In right field for the Yankees, Shane Spencer gathered up the ball and wildly threw past both of his cutoff men. If Spencer had hit one of them with an accurate relay, either could have turned and thrown to catcher Jorge Posada, waiting at the plate as Giambi steamed toward him. Instead, the ball skipped past first base along the first-base line.

To the disbelief of almost everyone watching the play, Derek Jeter appeared seemingly out of nowhere. He scooped the ball up and flipped it to Posada, who tagged out the stunned Giambi, who, to the horror of A's fans, remained standing up and did not slide to avoid the tag.

In the locker room afterward—the Yankees, with lights-out reliever Mariano Rivera closing things out, had won the game—Jeter calmly and patiently explained to reporters that New York actually practiced this defensive maneuver during spring training, a statement that A's third-base coach Ron Washington, who had waved Giambi home on the play, could not believe.

"Don't try to tell us you guys really practice that play in spring training," Washington said to Yankees coach Don Zimmer before Game 4 the next day.

"Well, if you don't believe it, then don't ask me," said Zimmer testily.

"C'mon," Washington went on. "Why would you practice a play where a guy misses two cutoff men?"

Zimmer explained that he had played some infield in his day and knew from experience on a ball hit into the right-field corner with a runner on base that the shortstop had nothing to do. So Jeter's job was to hang out around the pitching mound to back up the other infielders in case of an errant throw by the outfielder, as happened.

"Okay, I'll give you that," said Washington grudgingly, willing to accept why the Yankees shortstop might be so far out of position along the first-base line. "But how do you explain the throw being in the perfect place for Posada to put the tag on the runner?"

Zimmer smiled. There was only one reason for that.

"Derek Jeter," he said.

The Yankees came back in that Series to beat the A's in five games, then handled the Mariners in the League Championship Series. But the Arizona Diamondbacks ended their dream of four World Series championships in a row, narrowly defeating them in seven games.

After that Series ended, Yogi Berra, who played on five straight world championship teams for New York from 1949 to 1953, said to Jeter, "You guys gotta start all over again."

Sandy Koufax

When the Brooklyn Dodgers Baseball Club became the Los Angeles Dodgers Baseball Club and moved to California to begin regular-season play in 1958, its roster of players included such future Hall of Famers as Duke Snider, Pee Wee Reese, Don Drysdale, and manager Walt Alston. One other future Hall of Famer on the club, a left-handed pitcher, won a scant nine games with Brooklyn, flourishing only after being transplanted to southern California soil. He was the greatest Dodger of them all, Brooklyn or Los Angeles. He was Sandy Koufax.

What is interesting about the Koufax saga—well, there are many interesting things; this is only one of them—is that although his greatest years as a player came in Los Angeles, he was an honest-to-goodness native of the borough of Brooklyn, New York. A terrific athlete whose best sport as a youngster was basketball, Koufax played backup first base and pitched for the baseball team of Brooklyn's Lafayette High.

Larry King, the television personality, also went to Lafayette High and, like so many others from that time, marveled at the sight of the teenage Koufax on the mound.

"Occasionally he'd pitch, but he had absolutely no control," recalls King. "They'd warm him up in the bullpen to scare the other team. He'd be warming up, and he'd throw it over the catcher's head."

Despite his wildness (a persistent problem with Koufax in his earlier years, though not an unusual one for talented young left-handers), the

Dodgers thought so highly of him they signed him as a teenager to a bonus contract. From the Bay Ridge–Prospect Park League of Brooklyn (and one year at the University of Cincinnati), Koufax became a rookie major leaguer in 1955, and in his first spring with the club, some of the guys from the old neighborhood showed up at Ebbets Field before the opening game of the traditional Yankees–Dodgers exhibition series held at the start of every season in the days when both teams played in New York.

One of those guys was King, and he tells the story of how he and a bunch of other fellas brought matzo sandwiches to Ebbets to give to Sandy and his teammates. They crowded around the Dodgers' dugout, yelling for Sandy and advertising the fact that they had these delicious matzo crackers with chicken fat spread on them. The 19-year-old Koufax wanted no part of either the sandwiches or the guys who had them, but Russ Meyer, a journeyman right-hander for the Dodgers who was scheduled to start that day's game, happened to wander by.

King and his friends were all Jewish and had grown up on matzo sandwiches and the like. But Meyer, a native of Illinois nicknamed "The Mad Monk" (because of his fiery temper; once, after being removed from a game by his manager, he got so mad he picked up the resin bag lying on the mound and tossed it high in the air, the bag flying straight up and straight back down on top of his head), was not Jewish and had never tasted one before.

So, at the urging of the group, he bit into one and liked it. He liked it so much he ate one and then another and another and even called some of his teammates over to try one for themselves.

When Meyer took the hill for Brooklyn later that day, he gave up 11 runs in the third inning to the Yankees, who routed the home team. Herbie Cohen, one of King's friends who was with the group that day (and who would grow up to be a best-selling author), later claimed that Meyer's undoing was all his idea.

"It was my plot. I planned it," said Cohen, who, despite being a

Brooklyn kid, was a fan of the Yankees. "I fed him matzo and chicken fat, and no man has ever pitched five innings with matzo and chicken fat in him."

Koufax's years in Brooklyn were years of apprenticeship. Though obviously talented, with a fastball that went "whoosh"—in pitcher Ralph Branca's perfect one-word description—Koufax felt he never got a chance to really show his stuff. Brooklyn management used him infrequently and irregularly, and it frustrated him so much he even considered giving up the game.

When his roomie in Brooklyn, pitcher Ed Roebuck, heard him talking about quitting, he went to him and said, "Sandy, if you do, how about giving me your left arm?"

Stories about Sandy's wildness are legion; some may even be true. Dodger bullpen coach Sam Narron says he hated to warm Sandy up before a game because his pitches came in so hard and were so often out of control. After warming him up, Narron would typically walk away with bruises on his body caused by the ball skipping off his glove or bouncing off the dirt and then hitting him in the feet or shins or arms.

Finally, one day Narron decided to protect himself, putting on the full catcher's gear—mask, chest protector, shinguards—before agreeing to catch Sandy. Then he squatted down with his back against the bullpen fence at Ebbets.

Sandy fired over his head, too fast for him to get a glove on it. The ball ricocheted off the fence and nailed Narron in the back.

The breakthrough year came in 1961, three years after the Dodgers had settled in Los Angeles, when the no-longer-wild-armed Koufax struck out 269 batters in 255 innings and won 18 games, the most ever for him in a season to date. But his greatest year may have come two seasons later, when he recorded a major-league-leading 306 strikeouts and 1.88 earned run average, pitched a no-hitter (the second of his career; he ended with four, including a perfect game), and tied Juan Marichal of the Giants with 25 regular-season wins.

The Dodgers won the National League pennant that year and met the powerful Yankees in the World Series. Koufax won the opener, striking out 15 hitters to set a Series record and blowing away New York ace Whitey Ford. In the fourth and final game, Koufax and Ford again matched up and again Koufax came out on top, completing the sweep for the upstarts from Los Angeles.

After the Series, Yogi Berra of the Yankees, speaking perhaps on behalf of his overwhelmed club, said about Koufax, "I can see how he won 25 games this season. What I don't understand is how he lost five."

(Later, Maury Wills, the Los Angeles shortstop, would clarify: "He didn't. We lost them for him.")

The Dodgers of that era were a notoriously weak-hitting bunch, "piling up runs at the rate of one per game," as columnist Jim Murray noted. But with Koufax pitching for them, one run was often enough for them to win the game. He was that good.

After Koufax shut his Cardinals out in nine dazzling innings, Stan Musial said, "We couldn't have scored if we'd played all night." Pirates slugger Willie Stargell said that trying to hit against Koufax was "like trying to drink coffee with a fork." A reporter once asked Philadelphia manager Gene Mauch if Koufax was the best lefty he ever saw. "The best righty, too," said Mauch.

The ancient Casey Stengel, whose New York Mets played against Koufax and the Dodgers, said Koufax at his best was the best he had ever seen in his 50 years in the game. "Forget the other fellow," he said, the other fellow being Walter Johnson. "You can forget [Rube] Waddell. The Jewish kid is probably the best of all of them."

Like Johnson, Waddell, and so many other hard throwers, fastballs delivered by Koufax were said to be so fast that batters and umpires could not see them. Explained Casey, "Umpires often can't see where Koufax's pitches go, so they have to judge from the sound of the ball hitting the catcher's mitt. He's very tough on umps who are hard of hearing."

At Lafayette High in Brooklyn, the players in the field would sometimes sit down on the grass behind Sandy, because almost no batter ever made contact with the ball when he pitched. They walked or struck out; never managed a hit or even a feeble ground-out.

His Dodgers teammates showed similar confidence in Sandy in his prime. Although they never insulted the opposing team by sitting down on the field during a game, they fully expected to win every time he pitched, as did everyone who was associated with the organization.

One time, Jerry Doggett, the radio broadcast partner of Vin Scully, asked Koufax to tape an interview with him before a game he was scheduled to pitch, allowing Doggett to ask questions as if Sandy had just won it. The reason for this is that it was a getaway day and the Dodgers had to leave quickly after the game and Doggett did not think there'd be enough time to record a postgame interview with the winning pitcher.

Koufax agreed to do the interview as requested. Doggett asked all the right questions, Sandy gave all the right answers. Then he went out and recorded another win for the Dodgers, and the interview aired after the game.

Despite his mastery over hitters, Koufax threw only two pitches: fastball and curve. When asked why he never learned to throw any other types of pitches, he said, "Because I didn't have to."

Hitters knew what was coming—either curve or fastball, but most likely a fastball—and they still could not hit it. Koufax threw five straight fastballs past American League batting champ Tony Oliva, a dead fastball hitter, during the 1965 World Series between Los Angeles and Oliva's Minnesota Twins. Each pitch passed by him into the catcher's mitt (whoosh!), but Oliva did not swing at any of them because he wasn't sure if he actually *saw* them or not.

After the series ended (the Dodgers won in seven, Koufax beating the Twins in the final game with his second complete-game shutout in three days), Tony made an appointment to see his optometrist to check his eyesight.

"Nothing is wrong with your eyes," the optometrist told him after the exam. "You have the best eyes on the club."

Then how come he couldn't see the Koufax fastballs? For that the doctor did not have an answer.

Koufax's most lasting achievement, however, may be for something he did not do in that 1965 Series, rather than what he did. Since Game 1 fell on October 6, Yom Kippur, a sacred day of worship for Jews, Koufax declined to pitch or play. He stayed out of uniform and away from Metropolitan Stadium, where the game was held, possibly attending services at a temple in the area. To this day, Jews and others around the country express their admiration for his decision to honor his faith by sitting out the game.

With Koufax unavailable (he pitched the next day), Don Drysdale, the other half of the Dodgers' peerless pitching tandem, drew the starting assignment. But Big D did not have it that day, and the Twins roughed him up on their way to an 8 to 2 win.

The story goes that when Walt Alston came out to the mound to pull Drysdale in the third inning, after he had given up seven runs, the big right-hander handed over the ball and said, "Hey, Skip, I bet you wish I was Jewish today too."

Hampered by arm problems and pitching in constant pain, Koufax retired after the 1966 season at age 31. He earned induction into the

Hall of Fame five years later, in his first year of eligibility. Jokingly described by Milton Berle or George Jessel or someone (many claim credit for the line) as "the greatest Jewish athlete since Samson," Koufax lives in retirement in Florida, acting as a pitching coach and guru. A female fan encountered him one day and, in her excitement, grabbed his right hand, saying with near-religious awe, "I can't believe I'm with Sandy Koufax. All the things you've done."

As Koufax gently released his arm from the woman's grip, a friend who was with him said, "Lady, you ought to take his other hand. He's done more with that one."

Playing in a golf tournament in upstate New York after his retirement, Koufax met a boy from Lafayette High. The boy served as Koufax's caddy, and during the round he explained how much he loved to pitch and that his dream was to make it to the big leagues.

Koufax did not tell the youngster how hard this was going to be, how small his probability of success, how tough the competition, how many things conspired to prevent him from achieving his dream.

He said none of that. Instead, what he said was: "When you make it, be grateful."

Billy Loes

Billy Loes came off the streets of Long Island to sign with the Dodgers. This was back in the days when the Dodgers played in Brooklyn and Billy's signing bonus of $21,000 was considered a lot of money to pay a young prospect not long out of Bryant High in Astoria.

But the Dodgers figured the lanky, sweet-faced kid was worth it because he had a lively fastball and seemed instinctively to know how to pitch. What they did not figure on was Billy's personality.

Billy's first full season with Brooklyn was 1952. During spring training that year at Vero Beach, the Dodgers were running sprints to get in shape. Cookie Lavagetto, a former player turned coach, found Loes asleep under a tree.

"What are you doing?" said Cookie, stirring him from his nap.

Billy's eyes opened. "I'm a pitcher, not a runner," he said, and closed them back again.

Despite his less-than-rigorous work habits, the 22-year-old Loes won 13 games for Brooklyn that year as the Dodgers claimed the National League pennant. Their opponents in the World Series were the New York Yankees, who had won three world championships in a row and were favored to make it four. Loes agreed with the experts, telling a sportswriter he thought his club would lose to the Yankees.

Dodgers manager Chuck Dressen blew up when he read Loes's remarks in the paper, angrily summoning the young right-hander to his office. "It says in the paper here you picked the Yankees to take us in seven games," he said. "What's wrong with you?"

"I was misquoted," said Loes. "I picked them in six."

Surprising the prognosticators, the Dodgers took three of the first five games of the Series, needing only one more win to bring the title to Brooklyn. When the Series shifted back to Ebbets Field for Game 6, on the mound for the Dodgers was Billy himself, who pitched brilliantly for six innings and took a 1 to 0 lead into the top of the seventh.

But Yankees catcher Yogi Berra homered to tie the score, and left fielder Gene Woodling followed with a single against the suddenly rattled Loes, who, while standing on the pitching rubber, let the ball slip out of his glove to the ground. This was declared a balk and the umps gave Woodling a free pass to second.

After the game, when asked how he had dropped the ball, Loes replied, "Too much spit."

But that wasn't the worst of it. For Brooklyn fans, the worst was yet to come. With Woodling on second, up came Yankees pitcher Vic Raschi, who hit a hard grounder straight back to Loes. Loes missed it and the ball caromed off his leg into right field as Woodling fled home and the Yankees gained the lead. Mickey Mantle hit a home run the next inning and the Yankees won 3 to 2 to tie the Series. The next day, they beat the Dodgers again and claimed the fourth of what would be five consecutive world championships.

After that crushing sixth-game loss, reporters asked Loes how he happened to flub Raschi's grounder. "I lost it in the sun," he said famously.

Rebounding from the disappointment of the '52 Series, Billy came back to win 14 games the next year for the Dodgers. He reached this lofty total by the end of August, at which point he placed a call to Brooklyn general manager Buzzie Bavasi asking for immediate payment on his bonus.

"What are you talking about?" said Bavasi.

Loes referred Bavasi to his contract, which stipulated that if he won 14 games for the season, he would receive a bonus on top of his salary. Now that he had reached 14 wins, he wanted Brooklyn to make good on its part of the deal and pay up.

"Billy," the dumbfounded Bavasi reminded him, "the season isn't over."

"So? I get my money by winning 14 games. That's all I want." As Bavasi pondered how to respond to this, Billy went on, "If I win 20, you'll want me to win 20 all my life. I want to win 14. I can win 14 every year."

As logical as this reasoning may have seemed to Billy, it is likely the Dodgers waited until season's end to pay the bonus.

Brooklyn's manager during Billy's first two seasons with the club was Chuck Dressen, a venerable, talkative baseball man who liked to tell his players, "Hold 'em close, fellas. I'll think of something." Sometimes it was hard to think of what to say to Billy, but Dressen managed better than most. He gave the wayward youngster lots of leeway and encouraged him to keep improving his skills.

"Billy, you gotta take care of yourself," Dressen told him once. "You're a terrific pitcher. You can last 15 years in this game."

"I don't have to go 15 years," Billy responded. "I'm not getting married. I'll have all the money I need in five."

Just as the Dodgers were leaving to go on a road trip to Philadelphia, Billy heard that he was being sued by a woman who accused him of fathering her child. On the way to Philadelphia, and back again to Brooklyn after the series was over, Loes hid in the bathroom of the train to avoid being seen by a man trying to serve him with a subpoena. Dressen and his Dodgers teammates never said a word about his whereabouts.

Before each Dodgers game, the pitchers and catchers would get together in the Ebbets Field locker room to discuss how they were going to pitch to the batters on the opposing team. The Dodgers starter for that day would go down the names of the opposing lineup, one by one, and explain his approach to each hitter.

The locker room at old Ebbets Field, which has long been torn down, had large posts in the center of it. When they gave their pregame talks, the pitchers on the Brooklyn staff spoke in an open area of the locker room, away from the posts. All but one of the pitchers, that is.

When Billy talked to the other players, he sat behind one of the posts. Chuck Dressen let him do this because Dressen was an understanding man who knew that being superstitious was another one of Billy's personality quirks. Billy may have thought sitting behind the post brought him luck. Or he may have just been shy about speaking to groups. In any case, Billy wanted to sit in his chosen spot behind the post and Dressen let the boy do it.

So that was the scene: his teammates sitting in the open area of the locker room while Billy sat out of view behind the post, talking to them in that New York street-kid accent of his.

Billy retired in 1961 after 11 seasons with the Dodgers and other clubs. After announcing his retirement, he appeared in the Macy's Thanksgiving Day parade in New York.

Greg Luzinski

A major league scout was checking out a brawny, thick-necked teenager named Greg Luzinski to see if the kid's abilities matched his reputation. The kid was a stud, all right—Luzinski had been a high school football star, and looked it—but the scout didn't much like his swing or his supposedly vaunted power and said so loud enough for a Catholic priest to hear him.

The priest was sitting near the scout in the stands and, like the scout, was watching the game in which Luzinski was playing. But the priest could not let this piece of heresy pass unchallenged.

"My goodness," he said, referring to the hard-bodied Luzinski. "He hits them on the roof of that building."

The priest pointed to a building beyond the outfield fence. It was two stories high and perhaps 350 feet away.

"Since he was a priest," said the scout, "I knew he was telling the truth." The priest's testimony made him change his mind, and 17-year-old Greg Luzinski became a member of the Philadelphia Phillies organization.

After a few years in the minors, including one with the Reading (Pennsylvania) Phillies in which he won the Eastern League batting title on the last day of the season, Luzinski joined the big club for a few games in 1970 and a few more in 1971, which was the year Veterans Stadium in Philadelphia opened. In the shape (as many have said) of a concrete doughnut, the Vet was a modern, state-of-the-art multipurpose stadium that served as home for the baseball Phillies and the football Eagles.

On September 7, 1971, the 20-year-old Luzinski became the first Phillie to hit a home-run ball into the upper deck of the Vet—the first of ten such upper-deck blasts by Luzinski in his career. Phillies fans soon coined a term for these prodigious swats: "Bull Blasts," in honor of Luzinski's nickname—The Bull.

One of the longest Bull Blasts came the following year, Luzinski's first full season in Philadelphia, when he hit a ball that traveled some 500 feet and rang the Liberty Bell beyond the Vet's center-field fence. Luzinski's power was not restricted to Philadelphia. He was one of the few players to hit a home run into the right-field upper deck at Three Rivers Stadium in Pittsburgh (Willie Stargell of the Bucs did it three times), and later, after he left the Phillies for the White Sox, he reached the roof at Comiskey Park in Chicago three times, the only player to do so. "I just tried to make good, hard contact," he said, explaining his batting philosophy.

A member of the only world championship team in the history of the Philadelphia Phillies (they beat the Royals in six in 1980), Luzinski retired four years later, a veteran of 15 big league seasons. He coached for a time with the Royals and Athletics, and in March

2004, when the city of Philadelphia prepared to blow up decrepit old Veterans Stadium, it invited him to be one of the ex-Phillies to push the plunger that would symbolically bring down the building— "the final Bull Blast," as one reporter put it. The actual triggering of the blasts was apparently left to employees of Demolition Dynamics, the firm that oversaw the destruction.

It took about 3,000 pounds of explosives to bring the concrete doughnut down. Not just one explosion, but 2,800 different explosions did the trick. The stadium became a mess of rubble in some 60 seconds. Harry Kalas, the longtime Phillies broadcaster who was watching the event on TV, said, "I was watching and thinking 'Wow! All those 33 years of memories and poof! In less than a minute they all come tumbling down." The same could be said for Three Rivers Stadium and Comiskey Park, which have also been destroyed.

At Citizens Bank Park in Philadelphia, the new baseball-only park that replaced the Vet, Greg Luzinski operates a barbecue stand.

Greg Maddux

When they were boys, Greg and Mike Maddux played pitch-and-catch and hitting games in the backyard of their Dayton, Ohio, home, picturing themselves in the major leagues and pretending they were heroes in the seventh game of the World Series. But they almost certainly did not imagine what actually took place: both of them pitching against each other in their first year in the majors, Greg for the Cubs, Mike for the Phillies, the first time in big league history two brothers had ever faced each other as rookies.

The game occurred in late September 1986. Greg's Cubs beat

Mike's Phillies, 8 to 3, with Greg getting the win over his older brother.

In 15 seasons in the big leagues, Mike Maddux notched 39 wins (he's now a pitching coach for the Brewers), while brother Greg has gone on to record 300-plus victories and earn the praise of all those who enjoy a well-pitched game. "The best artist I've ever seen paint a baseball game," says Hall of Famer Don Sutton. Even Barry Bonds, who never met a pitcher he couldn't hit, expresses admiration for the crafty right-hander.

"For instance," he was telling a reporter, "Greg Maddux has 17 different fastballs. Hit the fastest one and you'll be okay. Simple enough. If you want to hit Greg Maddux, wait until you get two strikes. Because that's the only time you'll get that fastest fastball. He'll try to shatter your bat. Other than that, he's going to keep you off balance until he wins the game. The trouble is, if you wait to get two strikes, you're sitting in his kitchen. Just give up. Take your bat, drop it down, and just walk to the dugout, because the show's over. See, Maddux is like that little mouse that goes in the hole, out the hole, in the hole, out the hole."

Maddux may do this in-the-hole, out-the-hole stuff, but he almost never talks about it. He's a man of few words, frustrating feature writers everywhere. To a reporter asking him about his techniques and philosophy on the mound, he said simply, "I just pitch."

Everything with Greg is on the down-low. A splendid athlete who fields his position expertly and handles a bat pretty well for a pitcher, he once hit a grand slam for the Braves. A reporter wanted to know what he remembered about the moment.

"As I remember it," said Maddux, "the bases were loaded."

Leaving Chicago, Maddux came to Atlanta in 1993 in the early years of its division- and pennant-winning title run. Those were pitching-rich years for the Braves; besides Maddux, Steve Avery, Tom Glavine, and John Smoltz all started for the club.

But during one season Greg noticed that Leo Mazzone, the Braves' pitching coach, had come out to the mound to visit the other Atlanta starters during a game, but not him. Mazzone may have told Maddux he never came out because Greg didn't need his help, didn't need any advice, and that was why he remained seated in his usual spot on the bench next to manager Bobby Cox.

Nevertheless, Maddux felt left out and wanted Leo to come out. Not wishing to irritate one of his staff aces, Leo agreed to do it. Leo would know when to come out when Greg stared into the dugout at him. And so, in the sixth inning, Maddux peered into the dugout and Mazzone, realizing this was his cue, walked out to the mound.

Once there, he and Greg chatted a minute. Now apparently content, Greg said, "Okay, we've got you your TV time now. Thanks for coming out." Then Leo returned to his place on the bench.

After saying good-bye to the Braves and returning, in 2004, to the Cubs, the team that drafted and signed him as an 18-year-old, Maddux approached one of the most prized milestones for a pitcher: the 300-win mark.

Asked when he started thinking about achieving 300 lifetime victories, Maddux replied, "When I got to 299."

Upon reaching 299, Maddux missed on his first chance at 300, receiving a no-decision. But he got it on his second try, beating the San Francisco Giants at the Giants' home park in San Francisco. Afterward, the man who had supervised so many of Greg's backyard games as a kid, his father, Dave Maddux, said he was more nervous about the game than his son. "I was so nervous and so excited," Dave said. "I saw him after the game and asked him if he was nervous. He said, 'No, not really.' One of us had to be nervous. It's probably best that it was me."

To achieve No. 300, Maddux pitched into the sixth inning, leaving with runners on base. Cubs relievers finished the game for him, which meant he wasn't on the field when Chicago recorded the final out. In an age when it is common for games to be halted temporarily to celebrate some player's historic achievement, with these celebrations taking place on the field, Maddux stayed in the clubhouse after the game. He did not come back onto the field to accept the congratulations of his teammates. He did not do this, he said, because he did not want to embarrass the Giants in their home park.

Afterward, in the visitors' clubhouse, his teammates broke open some champagne, though Greg—"a man of little fanfare," as the Associated Press put it—did not party with them much. When the Cubs returned to Chicago, the club held a ceremony in his honor at Wrigley Field.

Mickey Mantle

In 1931, the St. Louis Cardinals beat the Philadelphia Athletics 4 games to 3 to win the World Series. The catcher for the losing Athletics was Mickey Cochrane, who, despite an awful series (he batted .160), was one of the best players of his time, widely admired for his intelligence, work ethic, and ability to lead men.

On October 20 of that year, ten days after the end of the Series, a mother gave birth to a baby boy in Spavinaw, Oklahoma. The boy's father loved baseball and was one of the many who admired Mickey Cochrane. And so he decided to name his son after him. His son's name was Mickey Charles Mantle.

Besides being a baseball fan, Mickey's father, Mutt, played the game, too. He played in the Lead and Zinc League of Commerce, Oklahoma, which was composed of men like him who worked in the mines all week long and then on Saturdays and Sundays wanted to breathe fresh air and run around on fields of grass, chasing a ball. Mutt wished for his son a life better than the one he had, and with this dream in mind, he taught Mickey how to play the game he loved.

He tossed the ball back and forth with him. He showed him how to catch with two hands. He showed him how to throw. He pitched the ball softly so Mickey could hit it. When Mickey got comfortable with faster pitching, Mutt tossed the ball in harder. Mutt insisted that his son learn to hit both ways, and from the earliest age, Mickey always took swings from both the left and right side of the plate. Little did Mutt know (his dad, Mickey's grandfather, also helped out) that he was raising the best, most powerful switch-hitter who would ever play the game.

Mantle was so good that at the age of 15 he was playing on the local junior-college team against boys two and three years older than him. Knowing it was against the rules to have a boy that young on his team, the coach told Mantle to never tell anyone his name or age, and if someone started asking him questions, just to walk away and not say a word.

The scout who signed Mantle for the Yankees was Tom Greenwade, who discovered him while on a scouting trip in Oklahoma. A well-respected and well-known scout in the Southwest, Greenwade was actually looking at another player but fell in love with the skinny kid (Mickey had not filled out yet) with thunder in his bat. "I don't know quite how to put it," Greenwade was saying to a reporter years later, "but what I'm trying to tell you is that the first time I saw Mantle, I knew how Paul Krichell felt when he first saw Lou Gehrig. He knew that as a scout he'd never have another moment like it."

★ ★ ★

Greenwade followed the teenaged Mantle for two years, worrying the whole time that some other big league scout would stumble onto him and sign him before he did. But no team could legally sign Mantle until after his high school graduation. On the day Mantle graduated from Commerce High, Greenwade, unwilling to wait a moment longer than he had to, made his move.

As it happened, Mickey did not attend graduation ceremonies because he was playing a game that day with the Whiz Kids, a local ballclub of talented youngsters. The afternoon brought rain, forcing the game to be postponed, and that was when Greenwade made his pitch to Mickey and his father.

They sat in the scout's long black Cadillac, probably with Mickey in the back and the two older men in front. Turning to present the boy in the backseat with a contract and a pen, Greenwade said, "How would you like to be a Yankee, Mickey?"

Mickey said, "That's what I've always wanted to be."

There was a hang-up, though. Mutt Mantle, who needed to cosign the contract because his son was underage, did not like the $140 monthly salary the Yankees were offering. Mickey could make more than that playing semipro ball and working part-time in the mines, he said.

Unable to negotiate on salary but knowing he could offer a bonus, Greenwade estimated how much Mickey could actually make in the mines and semipros for a year. The Yankees' salary offer, he calculated, fell about $1,150 short. So, to make up the difference, he offered a bonus of precisely $1,150.

They all felt that was fair, and the Yankees had one more legend to add to their all-time roster.

The young Oklahoman made a strong first impression in the Yankees' spring training camp. He was playing shortstop then, and although he had a strong arm, many of his throws were wild and he made lots of errors. But people reacted with wonder and awe when they saw him with a bat in his hands. "I've never seen such power like that," said retired Yankees catcher Bill Dickey, who had played with Gehrig and Ruth. "He hits the ball and it stays hit."

Not only that, Mantle was fast. He could motor. To borrow an old Branch Rickey line about Duke Snider, his legs seemed made of steel springs. In running races in camp that included all the fastest players on the Yankees, Mickey dusted them all, beating them by such large margins that the coaches thought he was cheating, jumping off the starting line ahead of the rest. So the coaches would call everyone back, restart the race, and Mickey would smoke them again.

His running time from home to first was clocked at 2.9 to 3.1 seconds, said to be one of the fastest such times ever. This speed paid obvious dividends when the Yankees shifted him to center field. As his manager, Casey Stengel, said, "This kid runs so fast in the outfield, he doesn't bend a blade of grass."

Billy Martin, then in his second year in New York, first saw Mantle play during the spring of 1951 when the Yankees held training camp in Phoenix. "Who's that butcher?" he thought to himself as he watched Mantle kick around grounders at shortstop.

Then he watched Mickey take batting practice. First from the left side, then the right, he hit balls that sailed out of sight. Which made Billy think: "Who's that show-off?"

Tommy Henrich, a sure-gloved outfielder who retired in 1950 after 11 mostly championship seasons in New York, returned to the Yankees' training camp to tutor the young Mantle on the intricacies of outfielding. He showed him how to get into the proper position when he caught a fly so that when he released the ball he could get his body and all of his considerable arm strength into the throw.

The student learned fast. During an exhibition game against the

Indians, Bobby Avila, one of the fastest men in the league, tagged up from third on a fly to medium-deep center. Mantle gathered the ball in and sent it on a line straight into the mitt of Yogi Berra, who tagged out Avila as he slid home.

"That was the most perfect throw I've ever seen in my life," Henrich told Mantle in the dugout after the inning. "You've got it. There's nothing else I can teach you."

With such great things expected of him—reporters dubbed him "The Phenom"; Casey called him "my phenom"—it was probably inevitable that Mantle would struggle early in his rookie season. Disappointed in his failure to hit, the Yankees sent him down to Kansas City, then a farm club in the New York system, where he continued to do poorly. This made Mickey get down on himself even more, and he called his father, asking for help.

Mutt drove to Kansas City and found his son, in a hotel room, in tears. He was doing so poorly, he told his father, he wanted to quit.

Mutt Mantle, who had worked all his life in the lead and zinc mines of the Southwest and never had anything close to the opportunities that his son was now threatening to throw away, had no sympathy. Angrily, he started collecting his son's clothes and tossing them into a suitcase.

"What are you doing?" Mickey asked.

"I'm taking you home," he said. "I thought I raised a man, but you're a coward."

That shook Mickey up. His bout of self-pity came to an end and he started hitting for Kansas City. In late August, he rejoined the Yankees and started hitting for them, too. He never played another inning of minor league ball.

Another famous (and poignant) moment in the Mantle saga came later in that season, during the '51 World Series between the Yankees and Giants. In center for the Yankees, in his last season in the big leagues, was Joe DiMaggio. Mantle was in right. In the fifth inning of Game 2, both DiMaggio and Mantle started going for a ball hit into short right-center. DiMaggio called for it and Mantle stopped suddenly, tripping on a sprinkler head in the grass. "My knee collapsed under me and I went down," he recalled. "The pain was so bad, I nearly blacked out. I remember hearing Joe say, 'Don't move. They're bringing a stretcher.'"

They carted Mantle off on a stretcher and took him to the hospital. He found out the next day he had torn ligaments in his knee. Coincidentally, the man who hit the ball was the only member of Mantle's generation who surpassed him as a center fielder: Willie Mays.

Mutt Mantle was in New York for Game 2. He left the stands when his son was injured and went with him to the hospital. Mickey was on crutches. While trying to walk, Mickey leaned on his father's shoulder. When he put his weight on him, his dad collapsed to the sidewalk. "I couldn't understand it," said Mickey. "He was a very strong man, and I didn't think anything at all about putting my weight on him that way."

The doctors admitted Mutt into the hospital, along with his son. But while Mickey could expect to recover, his father's prognosis was dire. He had Hodgkin's disease, then an incurable form of cancer. Mutt's father and brother had both died of Hodgkin's. A year later, it killed him as well.

After his injury in the Series and after learning about his father's illness, Mantle lifted weights in the off-season to build his body. This is another part of his story: how the once-skinny teenager became a 5-foot-10-inch, 190-pound, size-18-neck stud. "All muscle like an Oklahoma racehorse," said Walt Dropo, an American Leaguer of this era. "The more clothes he took off, the bigger he got." "He had the body of a god," said Yankees teammate Jerry Coleman, adding sadly, "Only his legs were mortal."

★ ★ ★

Possessed of a hard body, good-looking, friendly, with a soft Oklahoma drawl and a country (albeit sometimes crude) charm and innocence, the best player on the best team in baseball, Mantle was nevertheless convinced that he wasn't going to live very long, on the basis of the premature deaths of his father and other family members at relatively young ages. As such he played hard, often in pain and with severe injuries, and after the game was over, he partied hard, drinking copiously and nightclubbing into the wee hours of the morning with his good friends Whitey Ford and Billy Martin.

Casey Stengel said about them, "I got these players who got the bad watches—they can't tell midnight from noon." Martin, who roomed with Mickey for a time, was accused of being a bad influence on him and was later traded from New York because of it. In their late-night rambles, both he and Whitey matched Mickey drink for drink. Or tried to, at any rate. Some said it was impossible.

As Whitey once said, with a smile: "Everybody who roomed with Mickey said he took five years off their career."

In the second inning of Game 5 of the 1956 World Series between the Yankees and Brooklyn Dodgers, Jackie Robinson of the Dodgers hit a grounder that skipped off third baseman Andy Carey's glove. Reacting quickly, shortstop Gil McDougald picked the ball up and threw the speedy Robinson out by a step. In the fifth inning, Gil Hodges hit a line shot into the left-center-field gap that appeared headed for extra bases until Mantle ran it down and speared it with a backhanded catch. Those were the closest the Dodgers came to getting a hit that day, as Don Larsen threw the first and only perfect game in World Series history.

Mantle loved to have fun with his teammates and play practical jokes. Occasionally, he would arrange to have dinner with Joe Pepitone in New York. Pepitone, a young first baseman on the club who idolized Mantle, would eagerly agree to meet at a restaurant of Mick's choosing. Then Joe would show up early, only to discover that no such restaurant existed. His dinner partner, of course, was nowhere to be found.

Beloved by his teammates and fans, Mantle was not so beloved by the New York press, who covered him on good days and bad. Mantle distrusted reporters and was hurt by some of the unkind things they said about him, particularly as a rookie when he was breaking in with the team: "a hillbilly in a velvet suit," one writer called him.

One time, New York sportswriter Maury Allen was standing near the batting cage when Mantle was taking batting practice. Mantle noticed him there and growled, "You piss me off just standing there." Allen told his family the story of what happened when he got back home. The Allens then made the line their own, and whenever someone got mad at someone else in the family, he or she would say (often in a joking way), "You piss me off just standing there."

"He is the only baseball player I know who is a bigger hero to his teammates than he is to his fans," said teammate Clete Boyer. The reason for this was the injuries Mantle played with throughout his career. His right knee, the one injured in that 1951 World Series, almost had no cartilage left in it by the time he retired. His left knee was in almost equally bad shape.

Dressing next to him before an All-Star Game, Early Wynn could not believe what Mantle had to undergo in order to suit up. "I watched him bandage that knee, the whole leg," said Wynn. "I saw what he had to go through every day to play. Seeing those legs, his power becomes unbelievable."

In 1963, Mantle played only a partial season because of his injuries. His sprinter's speed was long gone. So, too, was much of his power. When he swung and missed, or checked his swing, he grimaced in pain and those closest to him saw it and felt for him.

Nevertheless, in 1964, his last good season, he played in 143 games and hit .303 with 35 home runs and 111 runs batted in. Mantle later said he wished he had retired after that year, but instead he hung on for four more seasons before quitting.

Mantle died in 1995 at the age of 63, the victim of alcohol-related diseases. After his death, a joke circulated around baseball circles. The joke has Mickey arriving at the Pearly Gates, whereupon the gatekeeper informs him that he will not be allowed to enter.

"Sorry, Mick," he says. "Because of the way you lived, you can't come in."

As Mantle sadly turns to go, the gatekeeper stops him and says, "But Mick, before you go, would you autograph these baseballs for me?"

Mascots

In March 1974, KGB Radio in San Diego had a promotion it wanted to do, but the promotion involved dressing a person up in a chicken suit and it could find no employees at the station willing to do this, even for a few hours. So the station turned its chicken hunt to the campus of San Diego State University.

There, KGB found only one interested applicant: Ted Giannoulas, a student at State who was working as a part-time dishwasher and busboy while attending classes. The job paid $2 an hour. No audition was held, no job interview. Giannoulas became a chicken by default because no one else wanted to be one. "Just show up," he was told.

Giannoulas did indeed show up, dressing in a rented red-and-blue chicken suit with a yellow-and-blue papier-mâché head. But a funny thing happened while he was handing out Easter eggs at the San Diego Zoo—actually, lots of funny things. A natural performer with a goofy sense of humor, Giannoulas found that while pretending to be a chicken he could make people laugh. Not just kids, but their parents too.

Thrilled (and no doubt surprised) by the reaction to their new hire, the radio station contracted with Giannoulas to make other promotional appearances. On Opening Day of the 1974 baseball season, he made his debut at Jack Murphy Stadium for the home-town Padres. And so the San Diego Chicken was born, or hatched. Of course, the chicken wasn't the first live-action mascot to come along. That distinction belongs to Mr. Met, who made his debut in 1964, and whose giant baseball head is described by the Mets website as having "its own gravitational pull."

Mr. Met remained a relative loner in the mascot community for quite some time. After the San Diego Chicken's breakthrough—a veteran of countless public appearances and a fondly remembered '80s TV show, *Baseball Bunch,* he's now known as The Famous Chicken—other mascots followed. The Chicken's best-known rival is perhaps the Phillie Phanatic, who began entertaining fans (or not entertaining them, as the case may be; one curmudgeon recently labeled him "a bumbling Muppet past his prime") a few years after the Giannoulas debut. Dave Raymond, the original Phanatic, has since bequeathed his 6-foot-6-inch green suit to Tom Burgoyne, who handles the job today. At Phillies games at Citizens Bank Park, he propels hot dogs into the stands with his Hot Dog Launcher, kisses fans, dances with umpires and coaches, and occasionally gets on the nerves of visiting players. The Phanatic has also rung the bell to open a trading session at the American Stock Exchange and written two books.

The Phillie Phanatic has donated one of his costumes to the National Baseball Hall of Fame in Cooperstown, as have two other mascots: The Famous Chicken and Youppi of the Montreal Expos. Pierre Deschesnes, a Quebec native who was the original Youppi, met his wife while performing as a mascot at a Montreal shopping center. While she was working at a store there, he kept talking to her and flirting with her while in costume. She so enjoyed his repartee that she invited him out to dinner. When they met that evening, it was the first time she had seen him out of costume. Deschesnes describes their meeting as "love at first sight"; they were married a year and a half later.

Youppi's debut at Olympic Stadium occurred in the early '90s during the years when such stars as Larry Walker and Marquis Grissom played for the Expos. A few of the players once played a trick on Youppi before a game, asking him to wait in the team bus until someone on the Expos came to get him. Youppi obediently waited . . . and waited . . . and waited, but no one showed. Meanwhile, the bus driver turned the heat up full blast, roasting Deschesnes in his heavy and hot costume. After about 90 minutes, someone finally let him in on the joke and ended his agony.

Deschesnes is not bashful about sharing his likes and dislikes among the players he dealt with during his days as Youppi.

People he liked: Reds shortstop Barry Larkin, (now) Red Sox manager Terry Francona, and almost anybody from the Reds or Cardinals.

People he "detested": Tim Wallach, in the last years of his fine career with the Expos, who apparently felt the same way about Youppi; Barry Bonds, George Bell, Tommy Lasorda. "Barry Bonds was detestable when he was with the Pirates, and he could be rude without respect anytime," recalls Deschesnes. Once, Deschesnes, posing as Youppi, grabbed George Bell's hat. Bell, then a White Sox, didn't like this and bopped Youppi in his big fake nose. Lasorda, managing the Dodgers, never liked it when Deschesnes came into his team's dugout. During one game, he asked the home-plate ump to eject Youppi from the game. The ump declined.

The most notorious incident in mascot history occurred in July 2003 at a Brewers game at Miller Park in Milwaukee. Mandy Block, a 19-year-old resident of South Milwaukee, posing as an Italian sausage, was racing a bratwurst, Polish sausage, and hot dog around the field as part of a sixth-inning stunt. Randall Simon, first baseman with the Pittsburgh Pirates, was standing on the top step of the visitors' dugout. He was holding his bat, waiting to pinch-hit.

As Block and the others passed by, Simon lightly swung his 34½-inch Louisville Slugger, knocking off Block's chef's hat and causing her to tumble. Block, who is 5 feet 3 and came up only to the waist of the sausage costume she was wearing, felt something jab at her. When she fell to the ground, she accidentally tripped the woman who was dressed as a hot dog in the race.

Both women gamely got up off the ground and resumed their race. When they finished, the fans at Miller Park gave them a standing ovation.

Dressed as she was in a sausage suit, Block did not see what hit her. Nor did Brewers manager Ned Yost, who was looking the other way when it happened. "I just looked over and saw our wieners in a wad," he says.

Though they did not see what happened, millions of people around the country did. That evening and for the next few days, television repeatedly aired the footage of Simon knocking off Block's hat with his bat and the two mascots falling down.

Many fans were outraged; others not so much. That night, after the game, Simon went to a bar in Milwaukee and the first thing someone said to him was: "It's about time somebody hit those sausages."

Local authorities and baseball officials were among those not pleased by Simon's behavior. After initially being booked on suspicion of battery, he met with the Milwaukee district attorney's office and paid a minor fine. Major League Baseball suspended him for three days.

Simon, a native of Curaçao in the Caribbean, apologized profusely and repeatedly. It was a bad joke that went awry, he said. He was only trying to tap the chef's hat, not knock anyone over. "I wasn't trying to hurt her," he said sincerely. "I'm really sorry about it." Later that season, Simon bought hot dogs for every fan seated in a section at Miller Park.

Helping to keep things in perspective was the good-natured Block, who refused to press charges against the repentant Pirate and accepted his apologies as well as an autographed bat from him. "I was just a sausage," she explained.

When the Miller Park sausage races resumed a couple of days later, the contestants made sure not to run too close to the team dugouts, both home and visitor. All those involved felt it was best to stay well away from the players, who, even before the Simon episode, had been known to spit seeds at the mascots and toss water on them.

The day after her accidental brush with fame, Block took the day off. When she came back to work she returned as a ball girl for the Brewers, shooting T-shirts into the crowd from the field. She appeared only once more as a sausage in a race at Miller Park, leaving the club the next year to study psychology at the University of Wisconsin at Madison. In the off-season, she received an award for bravery from the National Hot Dog and Sausage Council.

"I'm proud of it," she said. "I didn't even know there was a hot dog council."

Justin Miller

Justin Miller of the Blue Jays is the Illustrated Man of baseball. Lots of guys have tattoos, but nobody has 'em like Justin. To date, he has more than 60 tattoos, with surely more to come (after all, he's only in his late twenties, with lots of good tattoo years in front of him).

Justin is bald with a mustache and some fuzziness on his chin. Except for the numerals 5150—law-enforcement code for a person who is insane—tattooed on the inside of his lower lip, his head, face, and neck are free of ink. You cannot say the same for the rest of him, however.

About 20 of his tattoos are skulls and clowns. From his wrist up, his left arm is covered with ink. His right pitching arm, however, is mostly clean until past the elbow, where the tattoos on that side begin. Nevertheless, Major League Baseball requires Miller to wear a long-sleeved shirt to cover his arm so his body art doesn't distract hitters.

Two of his fingers say *Amor* and *Odio,* the Spanish words for love and hate. His son's name, Joseph, is tattooed on his chest, close to his heart, amid a swirl of designs that include a spiderweb, a woman's face, the words "No," "Man," and "Trust" in stylish script, flowers, and a pair of red lips above his collarbone. In the center of his chest is a skull wearing a hat. The hatband says 310, the area code for his old neighborhood in Los Angeles.

Lest anyone be confused about where Justin grew up, two giant block letters, LA, dominate his back. Between the L and A are more designs. Below the L, his last name is spelled out.

Miller's amazing bodily display no doubt caused his teammate, Blue Jays closer Billy Koch, to make a proposal that attracted considerable snickers during the 2004 season. He'd pay Miller $1,000 if Justin tattooed "I Love Billy Koch" on his rear end, the love being in the form of a red heart.

Saying he'd never do it on his forehead but didn't mind on his butt, Justin took the dare, got the tattoo on his right cheek, and earned his grand from Koch, who threw in an extra 500 bucks for Miller's wife. "She'll have to see that her whole life," explained Koch.

Miller said later his left cheek was available for sale.

Oriole Park at Camden Yards

"The smell of Camden Yards is baseball."

—Edgar Martinez, visiting player

Camden Yards may smell of baseball today, but during the Revolutionary War it smelled of men massing for battle. General Rochambeau bivouacked with his French army at the site on Chesapeake Bay in Baltimore, before marching south to join his American allies at Yorktown in 1783. The Battle of Yorktown, in which colonial and French forces fought the British for 20 days, led to the surrender of Lord Cornwallis. The defeat of the British at Yorktown essentially ended the Revolutionary War.

In April 1861, Confederate forces bombed Fort Sumter, a United States Army post in Charleston Harbor. Though no one was killed, the battle began the Civil War.

Not long after this, infantrymen from the Commonwealth of

Massachusetts who had been on assignment at Fort Sumter were passing through Camden Yards, which, with the invention of the steam locomotive, had been transformed into a major railroad center. These infantrymen fought with a group of Confederate sympathizers, causing the first deaths of the Civil War. The killing occurred near the present-day center-field bleachers at Oriole Park at Camden Yards.

Camden Yards became a connecting point for trains moving between the North and South during the Civil War. President Abraham Lincoln passed through it several times in his travels, most notably in November 1863 on his way to Gettysburg, Pennsylvania. Appearing at the dedication ceremonies of the new National Cemetery being established there after the bloody Civil War battle earlier that year, Lincoln spoke briefly and with simple eloquence, delivering the Gettysburg Address, the greatest of all American political speeches.

On February 2, 1895, the area around Camden Yards witnessed yet another piece of American history, though of a different and happier kind. A chubby little future home-run slugger by the name of George Herman Ruth entered the world and uttered his first cries at 216 Emory Street. When Babe, as he came to be known, was three years old, Camden Yards began a major expansion that made it the world's largest train depot, with more than 430,000 square feet of space. An already busy commercial and passenger rail center got even busier, spawning businesses that catered to workers and travelers passing through the area.

One of those businesses was Ruth's Cafe, a bar and café operated by George Ruth, Sr., Babe's father. Ruth's parents sent their seven-year-old child (apparently a bit of a hellion as a boy) to St. Mary's Industrial School for Boys in another part of Baltimore. Ruth went to school and learned to play ball there before signing his first professional contract at age 19. The address of Ruth's dad's old bar was 406 Conway Street. It no longer exists, but if it did, its patrons would have an excellent view of the goings-on at Oriole Park because it would sit in center field. A statue of Ruth welcomes passersby on the Eutaw Street Promenade outside the park.

With all its history, being only a couple of blocks from the birthplace of the greatest player ever, and just a short walk from Baltimore's Inner Harbor, Camden Yards seemed the ideal place to build a new baseball-only park to replace old Memorial Stadium.

With this goal in mind, the state of Maryland, led by Governor William Donald Schaefer, created the Maryland Stadium Authority to purchase the parcels of land that would make up the 85-acre site where the park is now located. Existing businesses were bought out and their buildings knocked down. In June 1989, construction began; three years later, it was done. The cost: $110 million. (And a real bargain by today's standards. Petco Park in San Diego, for example, opened in 2004 with a price tag of $458 million.)

Eli Jacobs, the owner of the Orioles at the time, wanted to call it Oriole Park. Schaefer argued for the more historic name of Camden Yards. They compromised, agreeing to its official name: Oriole Park at Camden Yards.

Opening Day at Oriole Park at Camden Yards was April 6, 1992. More than 44,000 fans, including Schaefer and other justifiably proud dignitaries, saw the Orioles beat the Indians, 2 to 0, as starter Rick Sutcliffe went the distance for the home team.

Camden Yards, in the words of commentator George Will, "aimed not to break new ground but to recapture lost ground." Unlike Memorial Stadium, which also hosted the football Colts, it was a ballyard only. It was not in the suburbs or on the outside edges of the city; it was in the center of the city, its urban heart. The park was not enclosed like a bowl; it was open beyond the center-field fence and fans could see buildings there, city buildings. Not only on the outside of the park, but also on its inside, the city of Baltimore formed part of its charm.

Oriole Park was smaller and somehow friendlier than multiuse stadiums built to accommodate larger crowds and other sports besides baseball. The design, by the HOK architectural firm of Kansas City, recalled intimate and funky (in a good way) parks such as Wrigley Field and Fenway Park, which were built in the early 1900s. The bullpen in left had two levels (a double-decked pen!) and the walls of the outfield fence featured eight different angles, suggestive of a place where different things happened, exciting things, where balls bounced crazily around as outfielders chased madly after them and runners tore around the bases.

Beyond the right-field fence was Oriole Park's signature feature: the B&O (Baltimore and Oriole) Warehouse built at the turn of the nineteenth century during the expansion of Camden Yards. More than 1,000 feet long, the warehouse is the longest building on the East Coast. Refurbished to contain the team offices of the Baltimore Orioles and other businesses, it stands about 460 feet from home plate, a distance as yet untouched by any batted ball during a game. Once, however, Ken Griffey, Jr., did reach the B&O on the fly during batting practice.

The first of the new retro parks, Oriole Park at Camden Yards changed baseball. After Camden Yards came the Ballpark at Arlington, Jacobs Field, Coors Field, Pacific Bell (now SBC) Park, and so many more. Its greatest on-field moment thus far came on September 6, 1995, when Oriole star Cal Ripken, a local boy who made good, played in his 2,131st consecutive game, breaking the former consecutive-game mark of Lou Gehrig, the fabled Iron Horse of the New York Yankees. In the top of the fifth, when the game became official, the proceedings came to a temporary halt as Ripken jogged around the field, shaking the hands of fans crowding along the stands lining the field. The cheering and applause were thunderous.

Three years later, also at Camden Yards, Ripken voluntarily withdrew his name from the Orioles lineup before a game with Gehrig's old team, ending his major-league-record streak at 2,632.

Shirley Povich

Shirley Povich began writing sports for the *Washington Post* months before the Washington Senators won its first and only World Series in 1924. This was in the era of Walter Johnson, the Senators right-hander who was perhaps the hardest-throwing pitcher of his time. Povich loved to tell a story—"undocumented but always well received"—about a game Johnson was pitching in the waning light of one Washington day.

Johnson's catcher that day was Eddie Ainsmith, who ran out to the mound to quickly discuss what to throw the batter on the next pitch. They had two strikes on him, but night was closing in fast (electric lights at ballparks were still two decades from being installed), and Eddie was worried that the game would be called on account of darkness before they had a chance to get him out.

"Listen," he told Walter, "this guy'll swing at anything, so wind up and go through your motion like you usually do, but don't throw the ball. I'll pound my glove, and it's so dark maybe the ump will think he didn't see it either."

Johnson did as he was told, going through his pitching motion but hanging on to the ball. Behind the plate, Ainsmith pounded his glove as if he had caught the ball.

"Strike three," yelled the umpire.

"That was no strike," said the batter. "It was a foot wide."

★　★　★

Two years after Povich's first byline appeared in the *Post,* he became sports editor, writing six columns a week while covering the daily beat for the Senators games. He was 21 years old.

Povich saw all the greats of the day, including Babe Ruth. Covering the 1932 Cubs–Yankees World Series for the *Post,* Povich was in the press box when Ruth, during an at bat in Game 3, pointed with his bat or perhaps his finger toward the center-field fence at Wrigley Field, as if gesturing to where he was going to hit the ball. On the next pitch, delivered by Cubs starter Charlie Root, Babe hit a mammoth home run over the center-field fence, close to the spot where he had apparently pointed.

People have been arguing ever since about whether Ruth actually called his shot or not. Povich, who was there, said no.

"He didn't really call the shot. He was pointing at the pitcher, Charlie Root, for quick-pitching him, and he was calling him names."

One day Povich was interviewing Casey Stengel, who liked to talk a lot. After listening to 30 minutes of nonstop Stengelese, a frustrated Povich interrupted him, saying, "But Casey, you haven't answered my question."

"Don't rush me," said Casey.

The son of Lithuanian immigrants, Shirley had nine brothers and sisters. He was the eighth youngest in the family, which accounted for his unusual first name. The Poviches were Jewish, and in the Orthodox Jewish tradition, children are named after family members who are deceased. But by the time his parents got around to him, all the boys' names (Abraham, Julius, Morris, Burt) had been taken. He was named after his grandmother Sarah, which in Yiddish is Sorella; this sounded close to Shirley, which was what his parents named him.

But in the early 1900s in Bar Harbor, Maine, where the Poviches lived, Shirley was considered a boy's name. In fact, he knew three or four other Maine boys with his first name. High school was the first time he encountered a girl named Shirley, which puzzled him. A girl named Shirley? How odd.

But as Povich was covering sports for the *Post* and later as a World War II correspondent in the Pacific Theater, this changed. Shirley became an accepted girl's name. So much so that after he returned home from the war he received a query from the League of American Penwomen, asking him to become a member.

The letter, addressed to "Miss Povich," began, "We have seen your articles and stories and have often wondered why you have not become a member of the League of the American Penwomen." Povich asked himself this question, and to tell the truth, he wasn't sure why he'd never joined, so he filled out the form: "Didn't tell any lies," as he said.

One question asked, "Has sex been any handicap to you in the journalism profession?"

Povich answered: "None at all."

Another question asked, "How do you get along with the men in your office?"

Again Povich answered honestly: "I only try to be one of the boys."

The League accepted him, only to later cancel his membership after learning the truth of his gender. Years later, Povich spoke to the Washington-Virginia chapter of the League of American Penwomen, proudly pointing out that he was the only man who has ever been able to say to them, "How do you do, fellow members."

The 1962 edition of *Who's Who in America* included a listing on Povich, who then received a questionnaire from the female version, *Who's Who in American Women.* Since this had nothing to do with him, Povich threw the form away and forgot about it.

The editors of *Who's Who in American Women,* however, thinking Povich was a woman, did not want to omit such an important personage from their book. They picked up the bio printed in the earlier *Who's Who* and ran it word for word in their edition, correctly noting that Shirley was married to the former Ethyl Friedman and they had three children.

Povich was the only man listed in the book; alphabetically, he came between Louise Pound and Hortense Powderman. When the press found out about the mistake, they had a good time with it. One paper ran his picture alongside two other honorees, Eleanor Roosevelt and Elizabeth Taylor. *Time* magazine showed him smoking a cigar.

"I was delighted and wasn't embarrassed at all," says Povich about the mention. "For years I've known it's no longer a man's world. I was glad to be officially listed on the winning side."

Povich, who died in 1998 a month shy of his 93rd birthday, represented a link between the days of Walter Johnson and Babe Ruth and the modern game. (Povich's son Maury is a television personality.) He wrote more than 15,000 pieces for the *Post,* one of his most famous being his same-day account of Don Larsen's 1956 World Series perfect game for the Yankees, the only perfect game in World Series history.

"The million-to-one shot came in," wrote Povich, punching out his lead on a typewriter. "Hell froze over. A month of Sundays hit the calendar. Don Larsen today pitched a no-hit, no-run, no-man-reach-first game in a World Series."

Later in the story, Povich described how Larsen did what no one else has ever done: "He did it with a tremendous assortment of pitches that seemed to have five forward speeds, including a slow one that ought to have been equipped with back-up lights."

Povich's last column for the paper, published the day after he died, compared Mark McGwire—"the St. Louis Cardinals' big-muscle Adonis"—with Babe Ruth. The crusty old baseball bard did not think the modern guy could hold the bat of the ancient one.

"To judge McGwire a better home run hitter than Ruth at a moment when McGwire is exactly three hundred homers short of the

Babe's career output is, well, a stretch," wrote Povich. To further illustrate his point, he recalled a quote by Walter Johnson, who, when asked to compare the home runs hit by Ruth versus those of Lou Gehrig, Jimmie Foxx, and other sluggers of the time, said, "Lemme say this, those balls Ruth hit got smaller quicker than anybody else's."

Kirby Puckett

Imagine what it must have felt like to be Kirby Puckett on his first day in the major leagues.

It was May 8, 1984. The year before, he had been playing Class A ball, the lowest level in the organized minor league system. Usually, a player must make at least Double A before being given a shot at the big-time. But the Minnesota Twins saw so much potential in the 23-year-old that they promoted him to the big club.

Despite his rapid advance, he was not your typical-looking ballplayer. Kirby was "built like a fire plug," according to one writer, packing maybe 200, 210 pounds on a 5-foot-8-inch frame—too short, according to some scouts, to accomplish much in the game. Puckett had heard such talk all his life. When he was a kid, because he was so small, the other boys always chose him last when they played pickup games at the Robert Taylor Homes where they lived.

The Robert Taylor Homes were another reason why Puckett had to feel good, real good, about putting on a Twins uniform with 34 on the back and stepping into the Metrodome for the first time. Not many kids from the projects ever did that. Located on the south side of Chicago not far from Comiskey Park, the Robert Taylor Homes were the largest public housing development in the United States, a true concrete jungle of nearly 30 16-story apartment buildings. The streets did not get any meaner than they did around there. People, nearly all of them of African descent, lived every day with the grinding hardships of poverty, unemployment, crime, and drugs.

"I'd be walking down the street, my bat and glove over my shoulder, and the drug dealers and the gang members would say, 'Hey, Puck, don't you want to hang out with us, drink a little?'" Kirby would recall years later. "I told them I had a higher calling."

Puckett's calling, his way to stay out of trouble and keep on a narrow path, was baseball. His family couldn't afford to buy him new gloves or equipment, so he sometimes rolled up aluminum foil and used that for a ball. He'd toss the crunched-up foil in the air and hit it with a bat. He taught himself to throw by tossing a ball—a real one, not aluminum—against the wall of his building. He drew a strike zone on the wall with chalk, walked off a certain number of paces, and imagined he was a pitcher striking out hitters who existed only in his mind. He played these pretend games by himself for hours at a time, as happy as a boy can be. Nobody coached him much when he was young; he never played Little League. Nobody played Little League at the Robert Taylor Homes.

Even with all this seemingly against him—the neighborhood where he grew up, his lack of coaching when young, his size, the color of his skin—Kirby Puckett had made it all the way to the Show. On his debut day in the majors he hit safely four times, tying a major league record for most hits in a player's first game.

In Kirby's first two seasons, he hit for a pretty good average but with little power—only four home runs in all. Then, in '86, help arrived in the form of Tony Oliva, a former Twins great hired to be the club's new batting coach. Oliva worked with the right-handed-hitting Puckett, teaching him to cock his left leg just before he swung, to improve his timing and to better harness the power of his telephone-pole thighs and robust upper body. The results showed immediately; he hit .328 with 31 home runs that season. Asked to compare Puckett with Rod Carew, another splendid hitter though without Kirby's power, ex–Twins owner Calvin Griffith said, "Kirby Puckett and Rod Carew both have magic wands. The difference is Puckett has dynamite in his."

Puckett's greatest game occurred in 1991 during the Minnesota–Atlanta World Series. Some think it was the greatest individual game in Series history. The Twins, looking to win their second world title in four years, trailed the Braves 3 games to 2 as the Series shifted to the Metrodome. In the bottom of the first, up against that year's Cy Young Award winner, Tom Glavine, Puckett knocked in a run with a triple and the Twins led, 2 to 0. But in the third, with a man on base, Ron Gant of the Braves drove a deep drive to left center as Puckett took off in pursuit. Leaping above the fence, he snagged the ball to take away a home run. In the fifth, after the Braves had scored twice to tie the game, Puckett's sacrifice fly in the bottom of the inning drove in a run and put the Twins back ahead, 3 to 2. The persistent Braves, eager to win their first-ever world championship in Atlanta, tied the game once more in the seventh and that was how it remained until the bottom of the eleventh, when Puckett connected for a game-winning homer. Not a bad day's work.

The next day, the Twins claimed their title and the Braves would have to wait until '95 to get theirs.

If October 26, 1991, was Kirby Puckett's best day on a ballfield, his worst day was surely September 28, 1995, when pitcher Dennis Martinez of the Indians hit him in the side of the face with a fastball. The pitch cut deep into the insides of his mouth and broke his jaw. Puckett never played a regular-season game again, although the reasons for his sudden retirement the following year apparently had nothing to do with the beaning by Martinez.

While in spring training in '96, he began to see spots obscuring the vision in his right eye. By the final day of camp, he could see nothing out of that eye at all. Doctors diagnosed him with advanced glaucoma, which causes blindness. After several eye operations failed to correct the condition, Puckett, a lively, upbeat personality who donated generously to charitable causes and was one of the most admired baseball men of his time, accepted the fact that while it is very hard to hit a baseball with two eyes, it is virtually impossible with only one, and announced his retirement from the game at the age of 35.

The press conference announcing his retirement came in July. Dressed in a Twins cap and uniform, Puckett wore sunglasses and a white bandage that covered his damaged eye. He spoke into a microphone to reporters while seated at a table with his wife, Tonya, who also wore sunglasses. She touched her forehead with her hand and at times cried when her husband spoke. Others in the room cried, too.

"I was told I would never make it because I'm too short," said Puckett. "Well, I'm still too short, but I've got ten All-Star Games, two World Series championships, and I'm a very happy and contented guy. It doesn't matter what your height is, it's what's in your heart."

Puckett directed his most poignant words to Dennis Martinez, who felt responsible for the premature end of Kirby's career even though people assured him he should not. The pitch he had thrown hit Puckett in the left jaw, while the glaucoma had surfaced in his right eye.

"I just want to say I love you," he said to Martinez, explaining to reporters: "He didn't do it on purpose. I was hanging out over the plate, cheating." For his teammates on the Twins, he added, "Don't take it for granted. Tomorrow is not promised to any of us, so enjoy yourself."

★   ★   ★

Because Puckett retired prematurely, falling three or four seasons short of 3,000 hits and with a relatively modest career home-run total of 207, some felt he might not make the Hall of Fame in his first year of eligibility. "If I get in," he told a reporter, "it will be a victory for all the short little kids who have been told all their lives, 'You can't do this. You can't do that.'"

Score one for the short little kids. Cooperstown inducted Puckett in 2001 in his first year of eligibility.

Since leaving the game, Puckett has recently encountered rough going: a bad divorce, charges of philandering, and other problems that have hurt his once-sparkling reputation and made his fans, particularly those in Minnesota, wonder about the man they had admired so much.

"Not that he is the only person in baseball or general society or the White House to cheat on a spouse," Jim Caple, who covered Puckett for many years on the Twins, wrote in a column. "Should I hold him to a different standard than I did the president? Than I do other players who have not had their dirty laundry aired in public? How do I feel about Kirby Puckett, a man who made me smile for so many years and now has left me shaking my head? Like a lot of people, I'm not sure. But that doesn't mean I don't feel for him."

Red Sox vs. Yankees, Game 7, 2003 American League Championship Series

The score is 5 to 3, Red Sox, bottom of the eighth at sold-out Yankee Stadium. One out, Bernie Williams on first. Pitching for Boston is triple–Cy Young winner Pedro Martinez, winner of 14 regular-season games with only four losses and owner of a 2.22 earned run average, the major league best. But New York has touched him for one run in the inning, and he is clearly tired, clearly struggling. At the plate stands Hideki Matsui, a left-handed hitter with a hot bat who is averaging over .300 for the series. But time is called as Grady Little emerges from the visitors' dugout and trots to the mound.

Will the Red Sox manager pull his ace or leave him in? This is the essential question, and how it is answered will decide the game and the Series.

In Washington, D.C., watching from a cloakroom in the United States Senate Building, Massachusetts senator and future presidential candidate John Kerry, a lifelong Red Sox fan, knew exactly what the Bosox manager should do.

"I was throwing things at the television set," he said, recalling that moment, "screaming at Grady Little, 'Get him out of there! Get him out of there!'"

Kerry agreed that the valiant Martinez should have been given a chance to start the eighth. But once the Yankees got a run in the frame, closing to within three with Williams on first and Pedro tiring, you had to pull him.

"When you go out to the mound, that's it, you get him out," said Kerry. "Everybody knew it. Everybody in Red Sox Nation knew it."

When he arrived to confer with Pedro, Little was joined by his infielders and catcher Jason Varitek, all of whom may also have had opinions on what should be done. But managers do not normally solicit the opinions of infielders in deciding whether to pull a pitcher, and Little did not ask them what they thought. They, too, were wondering what would happen next, as were Matsui and the Yankees, along with the 56,000 suddenly energized fans in the Stadium and the millions of people watching in living rooms and cloakrooms and other rooms across Red Sox Nation and the United States.

In his early fifties, with his gray hair visible under his cap, Little wore a blue warm-up jacket with an American flag patch on his right sleeve. His turned-down collar was red with white stripes, the Red Sox name with its distinctive red-and-white lettering across the front.

Pedro held the baseball in his right hand, his index finger and forefinger gripping the ball for all to see. Varitek and the infielders did not matter at this moment; they and everyone else were spectators. The only two people who mattered were the older manager and his great Dominican-born star.

"Can you get this done?" Grady asked.

"Let's do it," said Pedro.

Some observers have compared this moment to a similar one that occurred nearly 40 years earlier in the 1964 World Series between the St. Louis Cardinals and, once again, that team from the Bronx. In that game, the seventh and final of the series, Bob Gibson, who was the Pedro Martinez of his day (only better, one could argue), took a 7 to 3 lead into the top of the ninth for the Cards, only to be stung by solo home runs by two weak-hitting Yankees, Clete Boyer and Phil Linz.

With the score a suddenly much more precarious 7 to 5, Cardinals manager Johnny Keane came out to the mound to talk it over with his star pitcher. Having already pitched two games in the Series, losing one and winning the other, the hard-throwing right-hander was going on only two days' rest. Though clearly tired, Gibson, a man of commanding pride and dignity, surely did not want to come out, and Keane respected this. His decision, or nondecision, was to leave Gibson in, and it worked. The Cardinals pitcher held on to win, 7 to 5, and St. Louis claimed the championship.

Asked later why he let Gibson finish the game, Keane said, "I had a commitment to his heart."

It is certain that the '64 Series was far from Grady Little's mind as he returned to the dugout after his mound conference with Pedro Martinez. His decision to stay with Pedro has been criticized for being based merely on his gut instincts, not statistics—an "educated hunch," to use Grady's term—but for Little, at least, the numbers were why he did what he did. Several times during the season, he had taken Pedro out in the seventh or eighth inning of a game with the Red Sox leading, only to hand things over to a bullpen who then blew the lead and the game. Little did not want to repeat this mistake in the biggest game of the season.

But after Matsui stroked a ground-rule double to right, putting him on second and sending Williams to third, Little still had a chance to reconsider his previous decision as the switch-hitting Jorge Posada came to the plate. But Grady did not waver. His commitment to Pedro was, at that moment, total. With a count of two balls and two strikes, Martinez threw the hardest fastball he had thrown all night (it registered 96 mph on the radar gun), but Posada managed to get enough wood on it to hit a bloop single to short right, scoring both runners. The score was now tied, 5 to 5.

As Yankees fans nearly rocked the old stadium off its under-pinnings, Grady Little made the long walk out to the mound to do what he could not do before: take the ball from his courageous, but beaten, hurler. The Red Sox had finished second to the Yankees in the American League East, earning a spot in the playoffs via the wild card. After being down 2 games to 0 and coming back to beat the Western Division champion Oakland Athletics in their divisional series, the Red Sox felt that this year, of all years, might be the one they won the franchise's first world title since 1918. But as the van-quished Pedro departed, the hopes of the Red Sox seemed to depart with him.

In the months to come, Little would continue to maintain that he did the right thing, saying, in effect, that if you are going to get beat, you get beat with your best. "Time after time after time this year," he told one reporter during the off-season, "when this kid got into a jam in an inning where it's getting close to the end of his outing, he's the one we left in there to get out of the jam that inning. We got a bad result this time. Most of the time, we got good results. And he'd have gotten it done. What beat him was the bloop hit by Posada."

Tied 5 to 5 after regulation, the game lasted until the eleventh, when Aaron Boone's dramatic solo home run won it for the Yankees and carried them into the World Series. Shortly after the games ended, Little, back at home in Pinehurst, North Carolina, got the phone call from Boston management he knew was coming. He was fired. His tenure as manager of the Red Sox was over.

Relievers

"Almost every successful relief pitcher I know is a little crazy. You've got to be nuts in this job."

—Rollie Fingers, Hall of Fame reliever

American League reliever Marty Pattin was one of the best duck talkers of his time. Not only could he talk duck, he could sing it, too. Whenever his club traveled to Toronto to play the Blue Jays, Marty entertained his teammates by singing both national anthems—Canadian and American—in duck.

Will McEnaney, a native of Springfield, Ohio, got thrown off his high school team because, as he said, he was "an outgoing, mischievous prankster."

While with the Reds in the early '70s, the lefty prankster spotted a bag of balls lying near a policeman standing next to the visitors' dugout. (The Reds were playing that day at Jack Murphy Stadium in San Diego.) Rather than simply walk down and pick up the bag, McEnaney crawled through the middle of a 20-foot section of tarp that was used to cover the infield between games. The tarp extended from the Reds' bullpen along the first-base stands to the dugout.

After grabbing the balls without the policeman seeing a thing, McEnaney crawled back through the tarp to the bullpen, where his fellow relievers were rolling in laughter.

For perhaps obvious reasons, a Boston reliever named Wilhelmus Remmerswaal shortened his first name to "Win." One day the call came down to the Red Sox bullpen from manager Don Zimmer, who asked that Win begin warming up.

"He's not here," came the answer. "He's out in the bleachers buying peanuts."

It is not known what Zimmer's response was, but Win made only a few appearances in two brief call-ups with the Red Sox.

Al "The Mad Hungarian" Hrabosky intimidated batters not only with his power pitching but with the way he looked and acted. Between pitches he'd stand off the mound, facing away from home plate, swearing and muttering to himself. Then, when he felt ready to deliver the next pitch, he'd walk up to the rubber and glare at the batter, his fearsome Fu Manchu mustache in full view.

Asked why he wore a Fu Manchu, Al replied, "How can I intimidate hitters if I look like a damn golf pro?"

Hanging out together in the Kansas City Royals bullpen, Dan Quisenberry and Mike Armstrong used to pretend they were broadcasters doing the play-by-play of the game in Spanish.

"Of course," said Quis, "neither of us could speak Spanish, but that didn't stop us."

Quisenberry may not have known how to speak Spanish, but he did talk to baseballs, a not-uncommon trait among relievers.

"Have I ever told you about my agreement with the ball?" he was saying to a writer one day. "Well," he went on, as if actually talking to the ball, "our deal is I'm not going to throw you very hard as long as you promise to move around when you get near the plate, because I want you back. So if you do your part, we'll get to play some more."

One time Mike Armstrong and Bill Castro were warming up in the Royals' bullpen when the phone rang and bullpen coach Jim Schaffer answered it. On the other end was pitching coach Cloyd Boyer, who was calling from the dugout. Boyer wanted to know how Armstrong and Castro looked and whether one of them was ready to enter the game.

"Tell you the truth," said Schaffer. "They both look pretty ugly."

Phillies reliever Joe Rosa apparently does not talk to baseballs, but he does talk to trees. "They say you're suppposed to talk to them," said Rosa, referring to the new trees that were brought into the Philadelphia bullpen a few seasons ago. "So yesterday I introduced myself. They seemed to respond to that. It was a very nice moment."

One recent summer in Minnesota, the Twins couldn't do anything right, losing six straight games. In each loss, the bullpen had performed miserably. It got so bad that J. C. Romero proposed a radical solution for himself and his fellow relievers: Shave their heads. Get a buzz cut and maybe change their luck.

And so they did. The next day, the Twins took a lead into the late innings, but this time, unlike in past days, the relievers didn't blow it. They preserved the win, and the losing streak—also, their need for hairstyling products—was history.

Mickey Rivers

Miami-born Mickey Rivers played his schoolboy ball in Florida, where he developed the reputation that would later accompany him to the major leagues. At Dade City College, a game was about to begin but nobody could find Mickey, who was in the starting lineup. His teammates went out looking for him and found him near the park, asleep under a tree. In his full uniform.

★ ★ ★

Bucky Dent, who was Mickey's teammate in college and on the New York Yankees, remembers a practice at Dade when he was playing shortstop and Rivers was in center field. Bucky happened to glance into center just as Mickey was hopping over the outfield fence. Bucky learned later that Mickey had spotted some people arriving at the field that he didn't want to see, and he decided to hide out from them.

It's anybody's guess who those people were and what they wanted from Mickey, but a betting person might lay odds that it had something to do with gambling. Mickey loved to gamble, telling reporters that he always went to the racetrack on his mother's birthday. When asked why he chose that day, he replied, "Because the horses are running then."

About 5 feet 10 inches tall and skinny, Rivers broke into the majors in 1970 with the Angels, but he had his best years with the Yankees in the middle part of that decade. In 1976, he hit .312 with 184 hits and 43 stolen bases, finishing high in that year's American League MVP balloting. Despite these impressive totals, the Yankees felt they could get even more production out of their leadoff man, and the following spring asked him to learn how to drag bunt so he could get on base more. They also wanted him to be choosier in the pitches he swung at in order to take more walks.

Rivers resisted on both counts, saying, "I got my habits. I'm not going to change my habits. I ain't gonna work on my weaknesses, because it won't do any good. I build my strengths. I'm not gonna do nothing extra to please anybody but myself."

And that was that. Rivers did not bunt more as the Yankees wished, and kept swinging away at whatever struck his fancy. Mickey could steal bases with the best of 'em, but he just didn't have the patience to wait on four balls. In 1977, he drew only 18 walks for the season.

Asked once what his goals for the upcoming season were, Mickey said: "Hit .300, score 100 runs, and stay injury-prone."

Mickey was known by a few different nicknames: Gozzlehead, Warplehead, Mailboxhead. Another nickname for him was Old Man Rivers, a tag people hung on him because of the way he walked. His slow, hunched-over walk to the plate, dragging his bat behind him, reminded many of a tired old man, although a teammate on the Yankees, Sparky Lyle, said it looked more "like he walked on coals for a living." He also had an odd-looking left-handed throwing motion, and off the field he wore rhinestone socks.

Rivers was a key part of the Yankees' back-to-back world championship teams of '77–'78. Nevertheless, New York traded him to Texas the following season. Rivers said he was sad to leave New York because he had enjoyed his years there, adding that he expected at some point to be reunited with Yankees manager Billy Martin and owner George Steinbrenner.

"Me and George and Billy," he explained, "we're two of a kind."

Mickey finished his 15-year career with the Texas Rangers, amid reports that he asked to be traded from the team because the only thing to gamble on in Texas were cockfights.

Phil Rizzuto

Nobody thought Phil Rizzuto could play when he was a kid except Phil himself. Nobody that small—when fully grown, by a generous measurement, he stood 5 feet 6 inches and weighed 160 pounds—could ever hope to succeed in competition with boys who were so much bigger.

Phil's coach at P.S. 68 in Queens said as much when Phil tried out for the team there. He called him "a cricket" and stuck him in the outfield, far away from the action around the bases where a boy that small could get hurt. But Fiero—Phil's birth name; his father drove the trolley on the Brooklyn–Queens line—kept plugging away, and when he moved up to Richmond Hill High the coach put him where he had always wanted to be and where he excelled: shortstop.

Still, nobody gave the runty kid much of a chance. In those days, there were three major league teams in New York City. After high school, Phil tried out for one of them, the New York Giants, whose manager, Bill Terry, scoffed, "You can watch, kid. But you're too small to play." The Dodgers' manager, in Brooklyn, where Rizzuto was born, delivered a similar brush-off. "Go get a shoe box," Casey Stengel told him, implying that the teenager was only good enough, and big enough, to shine shoes for a living.

"You have to understand," Phil Rizzuto was telling the sportswriter Bill Madden, recalling those years when he was still trying to prove himself in the game. "In those days in New York, every kid wanted to be either a Yankee, Joe Louis, or go to Notre Dame."

Since little Phil was clearly too small to play football for the Irish or stand in the ring against the heavyweight champ, that left only one option: the third team in New York at that time. Fortunately for Phil (and for the Yankees, as events would prove), Paul Krichell, the scout with the golden touch who had signed Lou Gehrig, did not think the quick, smooth-fielding shortstop was too small to play. Rizzuto became a member of the Yankees' organization.

Scooter (so named because of the way he scooted around the infield) left Queens to begin his minor league career in the spring of 1937, heading south to a Yankees farm club in Virginia. The New York City kid had never been to the South before. When the train reached Richmond, Virginia, he got out to stretch his legs and have a meal. He ordered fried chicken, which came with corn grits, a grain dish much favored in the South. Phil enjoyed the chicken, but he had never eaten grits before. Heck, he'd never *seen* them before. Unsure what they were or what he was supposed to do with them, he put them in his pocket and left the restaurant.

Phil played three seasons in the minors and reached the big leagues in 1941. Despite his success in the lower levels—he won Minor League Player of the Year in his last season—he encountered plenty of doubters in New York. Among them were his new teammates, who wouldn't let him into the batting cage to practice his hitting in the warm days of a Florida spring.

"I felt it was me and 24 other guys," said Rizzuto, looking back on how the Yankees veterans treated him that first spring. One reason for their cool treatment was the fact that the 23-year-old was scheduled to replace the aging Frankie Crosetti, who had played shortstop for years for the Yankees but whose performance the previous season had declined miserably.

Finally, the leader of the Yankees stepped in to give Rizzuto a break. "If this kid is going to be our shortstop," Joe DiMaggio told his teammates, "we better let him get some swings. We're going to need him."

When Joe talked, which wasn't often, the other Yankees listened. They let the kid take his cuts. Rizzuto became the starting shortstop and hit .307 that season as New York won the pennant and the Series.

The first home run of Phil's career was an eleventh-inning game winner against the Red Sox at Yankee Stadium. In the emotion of the moment, fans poured onto the field and began circling the bases with the hero of the day. Most of these jubilant fans were kids, one of whom snatched Phil's cap from his head and ran off with it. For an instant Rizzuto, who, as sportswriter Robert Creamer points out, was "barely more than a kid himself," thought about giving chase to get his cap back. Instead, he let the kid go, and kept running till he touched home plate, where police escorted him off the field amid the crush of fans.

Later, Phil had to pay for the stolen cap. "In those days," he says with a laugh, "we had to buy our own shoes, our own sweatshirts, our own caps. [Yankees general manager Ed] Barrow made me pay for the cap, and that's a fact. I swear to God."

In September of Rizzuto's sterling 1950 season—he hit .324 with 200 hits, led the league in fielding percentage, and added the Most Valuable Player Award to his trophy room—some lunatic wrote him a threatening letter saying he'd kill him if he showed up to play against the Red Sox at Fenway Park. Rizzuto gave the letter to the FBI and told his manager, Casey Stengel, about it.

Rather than keep his star shortstop out of the game, Casey adopted a novel strategy, giving Phil's jersey to second baseman Billy Martin and letting Martin wear it while Phil wore one with a different number. "Can you imagine that?" says Rizzuto, who swears this story is true. "Guess Casey thought it'd be better if Billy got shot."

The death threat thankfully proved hollow, and all parties lived to play another day.

In the early fifties, in Phil's heyday as a player, his manager was a big fan. "What about the shortstop Rizzuto," Casey said, "who got nothing but daughters but throws out the left-handed hitters in the double play?"

When Rizzuto signed a contract with the Yankees for an annual salary of $50,000, big money for a ballplayer in those days, he posed for a gag photo sitting on Casey's lap. "If I were a retired gentleman, I would follow the Yankees around just to see Rizzuto work those miracles every day," said Casey.

Over the years, though, as Rizzuto's skills diminished with age, his manager became somewhat less of a fan. In late August 1956, with the Yankees comfortably ahead in the American League pennant race and looking ahead to that year's World Series, Stengel and New York general manager George Weiss felt they needed the left-handed bat of veteran Enos Slaughter in their lineup. But in order to obtain Slaughter, then with Kansas City, before the September 1 trading deadline, the Yankees had to release a player on their current roster.

Weiss and Stengel called Rizzuto into Casey's office and explained how they wanted to pick up Slaughter but needed to get rid of someone to do it. They asked Phil to look over the roster to see if he could suggest a player or two. Phil suggested a couple of players, but in each case Casey gave a number of reasons why they had to hang on to that guy.

Then it occurred to Phil that *he* was the one they wanted to release; he was the expendable one. Since this was before a game, Rizzuto was already suited up in his Yankees uniform. Once he realized the truth of what Stengel and Weiss were up to, he walked out of the office, shed his uniform, and left Yankee Stadium. His 13 seasons in the majors, in which he played only for the Yankees, were over. He never played another game for them or any other club.

That deeply discouraging day for Rizzuto was not the end of his career with the Yankees, though. A few days later, he got a call from WPIX-TV in New York, whose broadcasters, Mel Allen and Red Barber, thought the popular Scooter would be a good addition to the Channel 11 announcing lineup. Rizzuto agreed to give it a whirl, and a week after being released, he was on the air calling a game in which a base runner for the Yankees was edging off third.

Stengel had not changed the base-stealing signs since Rizzuto had left, so Phil saw that the New York manager had given the steal sign to the man on third. "Oh my God!" Scooter blurted out. "He's going to steal home on the next pitch!"

The Yankees runner did exactly that, and Scooter had a new career in broadcasting, one that he would continue for decades to come.

Like Jerry Coleman, another Yankees infielder of this era, who became a much-beloved announcer with the San Diego Padres, Rizzuto probably achieved greater renown as a broadcaster than he did as a player. His trademark expression of "Holy cow!" and his exuberant praise for the cannoli that family members and others would make for him and that he would eat while on the air, in addition to his unabashed loyalty to the Yankees, endeared him to fans everywhere.

Well, Yankees fans everywhere, at any rate.

On August 6, 1978, Scooter got word in the broadcasting booth that Pope Paul VI had died.

"Well," he said sadly, "that kind of puts the damper on even a Yankee win."

Phil could drag on as an announcer, however, and David Letterman talked about this tendency on his late-night talk show.

"I heard the doctors revived a man after being dead for four and a half minutes," Letterman said. "When they asked him what it was like being dead, he said it was like listening to New York Yankees announcer Phil Rizzuto during a rain delay."

As a former player and a representative of one of the Yankees' most storied eras, Scooter became a popular banquet speaker and baseball storyteller. One of his best stories involved his celebrated teammate Joe DiMaggio.

In 1941, Scooter's rookie season, DiMaggio hit safely in 56 consecutive games, establishing a major league record that still stands (and will probably stand for all time). The streak stopped July 16, when Tribe pitchers Al Smith and Jim Bagby held DiMaggio hitless in front of more than 60,000 screaming fans at Cleveland Stadium. Depressed after the game, Joe asked Rizzuto to hang out with him for a while. Flattered to receive such an invitation from the great Yankees leader, Rizzuto said yes, and the two men sat and talked quietly until the clubhouse emptied of people.

When they finally decided to go, DiMaggio realized that he had stored his wallet in a locked safe in the clubhouse. But the man with the keys to the safe had left with everyone else and Joe had no choice but to take off without his wallet.

Leaving the stadium, Joe spotted a bar and decided he needed a drink. Alone. Phil understood, and loaned him some money to do it. Then the two parted ways and DiMaggio went off to ease his disappointment with a solitary drink or two.

For the rest of that season, and again and again over the years, Rizzuto would tell the story of how he had loaned the great DiMaggio 18 bucks on the day his streak ended and how Joe had never paid him back. Finally, after sitting in the audience one evening at a banquet and hearing the story told one more time, Joe, by then in his seventies, approached Rizzuto.

"I'm tired of you always telling that," he said, offering some bills to Phil. "Here's the damn eighteen dollars."

But Phil refused to accept it. "I can't take it," he told Joe. "It would ruin my story."

Billy Martin always used to kid Scooter that the Yankees had held more days in his honor at the Stadium than anyone else, including Ruth, Gehrig, Mantle, and Berra. Not so memorable for Phil was the day the club gave him a cow. As Phil recalls, "The cow stepped on my foot."

"I'll take any way to get into the Hall of Fame," Phil was fond of saying. "If they want a batboy, I'll go in as a batboy." Rizzuto won election to the Hall of Fame in 1994—not as a batboy but as a shortstop. "I've had the most wonderful lifetime that one man could possibly have," he said in his acceptance speech.

Marge Schott

In the 1930s and '40s, when Marge Unneweher was a little girl, her father, Edward, a cigar box manufacturer in Cincinnati, used to bring her to his factory to give her a firsthand look at how to run a business. "Daddy wanted a boy," Marge said once, and her father nicknamed her "Butch." Edward Unneweher had five daughters and no sons, but of all his children he felt that Butch would be the one who could make it in a business world dominated by men.

She was the one with the head for figures, she knew the value of a penny, and she would not sit quietly by if she saw something she did not like. She always spoke her peace, even if it irritated people at times.

Little did Edward know that a half-century later Butch would enter what she described as "the old boys' club" of major league baseball and become owner of the Cincinnati Reds.

★ ★ ★

Before entering major league baseball, Marge Unneweher met and married Charles Schott, taking his last name. Charles Schott, who owned Schott Buick and other car dealerships in the Cincinnati area, was a big baseball fan, and for many years he and Marge—everyone knew her as Marge, simply Marge—hosted an annual Reds Rally, as it was called, at their 70-acre estate in Indian Hill. The charity event included an auction and dinner with personal appearances by Reds players, and over the years it raised more than $1 million for Children's Hospital in Cincinnati.

This could have been Marge's life—wife of a wealthy businessman, hosting charity events, entertaining at their Tudor mansion—were it not for the sudden death of her husband from a heart attack in the late 1960s. When Charles died, he left her an estate valued at more than $3 million, including Schott Buick. Tragically, unexpectedly, then not quite 40 years old, Edward Unneweher's second-born daughter had to apply the business lessons she had learned as a young girl.

General Motors wanted to strip her of her late husband's Buick dealership, but Marge fought back and retained control, becoming the first woman owner of a GM dealership in a city in the United States.

When, years later, she became a limited partner of the Reds, the greeting she received from baseball was about as warm as the one she initially got from GM. But the cause of this acrimony was partly her own doing, owing to her habit of saying whatever was on her mind, even if what was on her mind should have never been said.

In the early eighties, when she owned only a minority stake in the team, the Reds finished last in the National League West in 1982 and 1983, and second-to-last in 1984. The glory days of the Big Red Machine were long gone, the club was sputtering and inept, and, as the old saying goes, fans were staying away from Riverfront Stadium in droves.

Marge blamed this rotten state of affairs on Reds general manager Dick Wagner.

"If they want to fill the stadium, they should have an I Don't Like Dick Wagner Night," she said. When asked if she herself would attend a night of this kind, she replied, "I don't think I'd be able to get in."

Joe Morgan, Tony Perez, and Pete Rose all starred for Cincinnati's Big Red Machine, one of the best baseball teams ever. But they had long said good-bye to the city and by 1983 were all plying their trade for Philadelphia. When the Phillies visited Riverfront for a series against the Reds, Marge hired a plane to fly a banner above the stadium. The banner read, "Tony, Pete, Joe. Help . . . Love, Marge."

Pete Rose did, in fact, return to the Reds the following year as player-manager, and he and Marge, both Cincinnati natives, got along famously. "The Pete and Marge Show," the wags called it, and it injected some pizzazz into a franchise in sorry need of it.

But Marge's affection for Pete, which was vast, had its limits. Once when he was visiting her at her home, her large and lumbering St. Bernard dog, Schottzie, drooled on him.

When Rose objected, Marge said, "The dog lives here, Pete. You're just visiting."

After Charles died, Marge never remarried, living by herself in her Indian Hill mansion with her beloved Schottzie, who became the team mascot after Marge became president and general partner of the Reds and assumed full control of the club. She never went anywhere without Schottzie, who was truly the owner's pet. He was known to relieve himself on the synthetic-turf playing field at Riverfront, and the story goes that Reds general manager Bob Quinn (her nemesis Dick Wagner was long gone by this point) once had to clean up Schottzie's poop in the team's executive offices.

★ ★ ★

Writers labeled her "outspoken," and she was. "Pitchers are boring," she said. "I want to see home runs." Though she was an enthusiastic and loyal rooter, her knowledge of the game was sometimes lacking. "Is Kansas City in our division?" she asked. She wondered why there were so many scouts on the Reds' payroll, when they didn't appear to do much of anything. "All scouts do is watch games," she said.

She drank vodka and chain-smoked Carlton cigarettes, addressing all she met as "Honey," whether they were man or woman. "She was a crusty old broad," said Reds broadcaster Marty Brennaman, "and I say that affectionately."

And in 1990, after hiring Lou Piniella to replace Rose as manager, this crusty old broad helped bring a world championship back to Cincinnati.

Even her staunchest critics give Marge credit for opening up her pocketbook to acquire the kind of talent that could sweep the favored Oakland Athletics in four games in the '90 Series. These Reds starred dazzling shortstop Barry Larkin, equally dazzling center fielder Eric Davis, and the fabled Nasty Boys in the bullpen—Rob Dibble, Norm Charlton, Randy Myers. But that Series also showed Marge could squeeze a penny tighter than almost anybody.

Gamely playing (and playing well) despite shoulder and leg injuries, Eric Davis lacerated a kidney while diving for a ball in the outfield in the fourth and final game. Forced to leave the game to go to the hospital, Davis later flew from Oakland to his home in Los Angeles to receive additional care. But the bill was on him; Marge refused to pay for the flight.

Similarly, after clinching the Series and celebrating in the locker room of the Coliseum, the jubilant Reds shuttled across the bay to the Parc 55 Hotel in San Francisco, where they were staying. But Marge had sent the hotel's kitchen staff home early in order to save money. So Lou Piniella and outfielder Billy Hatcher went out and bought hamburgers at a fast-food joint and brought them back for the team.

Marge's frugality was the stuff of legend. She supposedly watched over the amount of paper clips being used in the Reds' front office. She turned off copy machines that were not in use and lights in offices when no one was in them. She required that scouts, not her favorite group to begin with, stop making calls from hotel rooms because of the high service charges placed on these calls. It is said she sold day-old doughnuts to fans waiting in line to buy tickets to Reds games.

To her way of thinking, such austerity made sense. She wanted to keep ticket prices down so that families and average fans could afford to come to Riverfront and eat dollar hot dogs, another firmly held conviction of hers. Hot dogs were a buck, always a buck, when she owned the team.

Despite her reputation for thrift, Marge spent generously to get good players for the Reds—a trait noted and appreciated by Cincinnati fans—and donated six-figure sums to the zoo, medical research, boys' and girls' clubs, and other charitable causes— another trait of hers that did not escape local notice. If someone tried to praise her for her largesse, she'd take another drag on her Carlton and wave them away, saying dismissively, "It's only money, honey."

And yet for all her good works there was Marge, speaking up when she should have kept her mouth shut, saying bad things about blacks. As a result, baseball suspended her from the game for a year in 1993. Six years later, after being censured for more ill-considered remarks (this time about Adolf Hitler), she sold the Reds for $67 million, a sizable portion of which she donated to charity before her death in 2004.

"I guess I always thought of her as a tragic figure," said Fay Vincent, who served as commissioner of baseball partly during the years Schott owned the Reds. "She tried very hard to do the right things for baseball, but she had enormous limitations and she had some difficulty overcoming them."

Following her death, Cincinnati and the Reds paid tribute to Schott at the Findlay Market Parade, the city's annual downtown celebration of Opening Day and the arrival of a new baseball season.

61*

Before Barry chased and passed Mark, and before Mark and Sammy chased and passed Roger, Roger and Mickey chased the Babe. Roger was Roger Maris, of course, and Mickey was Mickey Mantle, but in that historic home-run race of 1961, only one of them broke Babe Ruth's long-standing single-season record for most home runs in a season—and it wasn't Mickey. It was Roger, and therein lies the story.

Born in Hibbing, Minnesota, and raised in Fargo, North Dakota, the 22-year-old Maris broke into the majors with the Cleveland Indians. A solid 6-foot, 200-pound outfielder, he combined home-run pop in his bat with a real stubborn streak and a habit for saying the wrong thing at the wrong time. Cleveland traded him to Kansas City, who then traded him to New York, where his talents blossomed. Hitting third in front of Mickey Mantle in the formidable Yankees lineup, Maris—his manager, Casey Stengel, said he had "more power than Stalin"—hit 39 home runs with 112 RBIs to win the 1960 American League Most Valuable Player Award.

The craziness began the next season. "I just wanted to be one of the guys, an average player having a good season," said Maris. But when he and Mantle started having not just a good year but a great year, vying against each other to break one of the most revered records in baseball history—Ruth's 1927 mark of 60 home runs in a season—being an average guy was no longer possible.

Roger started slowly, hitting only one home run in April. But his pace quickened after that. By May's end, he had 12; by June's end, 27. Thirteen more followed in July and another 11 in August to bring him to 51. With a month to go in the season, he was closing in on Ruth's mark, even as his teammate and closest competitor was about to experience one of the bad pieces of luck that characterized his brilliant but injury-marred career.

In September, Mantle suffered an infection that forced him to miss a number of games and many precious at bats. Consequently, his once-torrid home-run pace slowed, and he fell too far behind to catch Ruth. Much of the fan and media attention then shifted to Maris, who was not prepared for it.

Mantle was the popular one, the true Yankee, the genuine home-run slugger, while Maris was seen as a Johnny-come-lately who hit cheap dingers that barely cleared Yankee Stadium's short right-field porch. The reporters crowding around his locker after every game regarded him as surly and hostile, and some of the things the blunt-spoken Maris said only aggravated the situation.

"It's a business," he said about baseball. "If I could make more money down in the zinc mines, I'd be mining zinc."

A wannabe zinc miner surpassing the immortal Ruth? Many longtime fans detested the idea of this, disliked Maris personally, and "some of the things yelled at him were the roughest I ever heard," said Mantle.

Maris was under so much pressure that his hair started falling out of his head. He went to a doctor to see what was wrong, and the doctor told him not to worry. Nerves and stress were causing the hair loss.

After the season ended and the pressure eased off, his hair would grow back.

In 1961, the American League expanded from eight to ten teams and increased its schedule of games from 154 to 162. Ruth hit his 60 in 154 games, which prompted a debate over whether 61 home runs hit in 162 games should be regarded as actually "breaking" the record. Commissioner Ford Frick issued his famous (or infamous) opinion, declaring that if Maris took more than 154 games to pass Ruth, this new mark would have an asterisk attached in the record books, stipulating that it was achieved during a longer schedule.

After 153 games Maris had 58 home runs, two shy of Ruth. If he was going to tie Ruth's mark in 154 games, which he dearly wanted to do, he needed to hit two home runs in a September 20 night game at Baltimore, where Ruth, coincidentally, was born and raised. In his second at bat, Maris hit a 400-foot homer to right, giving him 59. But in his next two trips to the plate he struck out and flied out, leaving him with one more chance as he came up to bat in the ninth inning against venerable Orioles knuckleballer Hoyt Wilhelm.

Wilhelm, who is in the Hall of Fame, sucked all the drama out of the confrontation by getting Maris to hit a check-swing grounder back to him on the mound, and Ruth's 154-game mark was safe. Maris had to wait to hit No. 60 in his 158th game, and No. 61, the record-breaker, came on the last day of the season.

Though he wasn't at Yankee Stadium to see Maris break the record that day, Billy Crystal avidly followed the home-run chase that summer and fall. As a 14-year-old kid growing up on Long Island, New York, he lived for the Yankees.

Billy's father ran a record store on Forty-second Street in Manhattan, and his uncle Milt Gabler was a well-known record producer who had founded Commodore Records and Decca Records. One of the hits on the Decca label, produced by Billy's uncle Milt, was the Bill Haley rock anthem "(We're Gonna) Rock Around the Clock."

Growing up in such a talented family, the funny and outgoing Crystal turned out to have a bit of talent himself, becoming a comedian and later starring on *Saturday Night Live* and in such movies as *When Harry Met Sally* and *City Slickers,* which he cowrote. The scene in *City Slickers* in which Crystal's character reminisces about the best day of his life—the day his father took him to Yankee Stadium for the first time—was based on Crystal's own life.

And in 2000, fulfilling a long-held dream of his, Crystal began production on a new TV movie, *61**, based on the Roger Maris saga.

Crystal had found the actor who would play Maris, Barry Pepper, while watching a screening of *Saving Private Ryan*, in which Pepper played a sniper in World War II. Pepper bore an uncanny facial resemblance to the real-life Maris, who had died years earlier. Problem was, Pepper didn't play a lick of baseball.

Nor, for that matter, did the blond, good-looking Thomas Jane, the actor chosen to play Mickey Mantle.

Enter Reggie Smith, the former Dodgers and Red Sox star who ran an instructional batting clinic in southern California and who entered the big leagues just as Mantle and Maris were leaving. His charge was to turn Pepper and Jane into facsimiles of ballplayers, and he was given eight weeks to do it, the goal being to get them good enough so they could do their playing scenes themselves, without stand-ins.

Pepper had an advantage in that Maris hit left-handed, so he only had to learn to hit that way. But Mantle hit from both sides of the plate, so Jane needed to become a switch-hitter. It took Jane a little longer than Pepper to get into the swing of things, but once he did, the two developed a friendly rivalry, seeing which could outdo the other. Smith encouraged this, because Mantle and Maris had the same sort of home-run-hitting rivalry.

★   ★   ★

Besides learning how to hit, Barry Pepper tried to learn everything he could about Maris the man in order to get into his character. Roger trimmed the sleeves on his Yankee jersey in order to show off his sizable biceps. Barry did the same. Barry lifted weights before production and even between scenes to build up his muscles to resemble Roger's. He also left the top button of his jersey unbuttoned the way Roger did.

Roger loved to play a board game called Labyrinth, and Barry learned the game to gain insight into Roger's personality. Barry does not smoke, but since Roger smoked tobacco, Barry smoked unfiltered cigarettes during filming, even though they made him sick.

Billy Crystal wanted to be as accurate as possible when re-creating the early 1960s. As befitting a ballplayer of his caliber, Maris played with a Roger Maris–endorsed glove, which Spalding had not manufactured for probably three decades. But the production staff dug up an authentic Maris glove that Pepper used in the movie.

In other areas, the real thing gave way to Hollywood's version of it. Topps baseball cards featuring the real Maris were not used; rather, they were reproductions of cards with Barry's picture on the front in place of Roger's. What was supposed to be Yankee Stadium in the movie was actually Detroit's Tiger Stadium with a digitally created Bronx landscape in the background. Memorial Coliseum in Baltimore, the site of Roger's duel with Hoyt Wilhelm, was in fact Memorial Coliseum in Los Angeles. Longtime major league knuckleballer Tom Candiotti played Wilhelm.

For that dramatic moment, the moviemakers wanted to simulate the arrival of a hurricane on the East Coast. But the wind machine that was supposed to shake the trees wasn't moving them around enough. So some members of the production crew climbed into the trees and began shaking the branches themselves. This did the trick, and the shooting continued.

★   ★   ★

The movie required about 400 extras to fill a lower section of Tiger Stadium. Many of the crowd shots were digital creations, but director Crystal wanted real people in the stands sitting behind Pepper or Jane when they came to bat. When the camera angle changed, the extras would stand up and move to another section so that it appeared every seat was filled. Except for the extras in their seats, the park was empty.

Crystal asked an extra with a Fu Manchu to be removed from the stands because those types of mustaches were seldom seen in 1961 and it was unlikely that a fan wearing one would have been watching the home-run chase. But rather than lose his place in the movie, the man with the Fu Manchu asked for and received a razor, shaving his mustache off while remaining in his seat.

Fans at ballgames obviously cheer after players hit home runs or pitchers get them out, which created a problem for the moviemakers. The cheers of the crowd made it impossible to hear the dialogue being spoken by Pepper, Jane, and others in the cast. So the extras in the seats opened their mouths wide as if to yell, but remained silent.

A bigger problem was applause. When people yell they also clap, but to not touch your hands when you are supposedly clapping looks fake. So all the extras clapped by bringing only the heels of their hands together, not their fingers or palms, which hardly makes a sound.

Mickey Mantle—the real-life Mickey Mantle—admired Roger Maris because he kept hitting home runs in the final month of the '61 season, even with so much pressure on him. "Every time you come to bat that last month, everyone is anticipating a home run, and you know it," said Mickey. "You start to tighten up. You start trying too hard. And you lose your rhythm and timing."

The same thing happened, on a minor scale, to Barry Pepper, who was supposed to lift a deep fly into right at Tiger Stadium as if

Roger Maris had just hit a home run at Yankee Stadium. But Pepper couldn't do it. He kept fouling off pitches and hitting weak grounders and pop-ups.

After thirty minutes of this, the extras in the seats started to boo. "It was amazing," said Reggie Smith, who was there. "The extras were actually getting on him." As Pepper felt the heat from the fans, the strain on his face showed, and he tightened up.

Roger Maris's 61st home run of the 1961 season, hit off Red Sox right-hander Tracy Stallard at Yankee Stadium, traveled about 340 feet. Those on the set of *61** swear that the ball Barry Pepper hit that was Maris's 61st home run in the movie traveled more than 300 feet.

Souvenir Balls

It is common knowledge (at least among serious baseball buffs) that Tracy Stallard threw the ball that Roger Maris hit for his 61st home run of the 1961 season, breaking Babe Ruth's long-standing single-season homer mark. But who was the fan at Yankee Stadium who caught it? The answer, not so commonly known, was Sal Durante.

Durante apparently later sold the ball to a man from Sacramento, California, Sam Gordon, who gave it to Maris. Roger in turn donated it to the Baseball Hall of Fame in Cooperstown.

Henry Aaron hit another famous home-run ball that broke another of Ruth's famous records, his lifetime homer mark. While pursuing Ruth's record, Aaron, who is black, received more than 900,000 letters, including many that insulted him because of the color of his skin. Some even threatened violence if he surpassed the legendary Ruth, who was white. The FBI confiscated the most threatening letters and provided Aaron with protection as he finished the 1973 season with 713 home runs, one behind Ruth.

On Opening Day of the 1974 season in Cincinnati, in his first at bat, Aaron hit No. 714 off the Reds. With his quest shifting to Atlanta's Fulton County Stadium a few days later, he came up in the fourth inning with two men on base. Left-hander Al Downing was pitching for the Dodgers, who were leading 4 to 1. At precisely 9:07 P.M., Aaron crunched a low slider into the bullpen beyond the left-field fence for the record-breaker, which also tied the game. Under pressure for so long, a quiet man unaccustomed to having the spotlight focused so intently on him, Aaron, clearly relieved, rounded the bases while being pursued by some fans who had run onto the field in the excitement of the moment. His teammates greeted him with joy when he touched home plate. His mother came onto the field and embraced him, too.

Out in the bullpen, Tom House, a reliever with the Braves, retrieved No. 715. House's only thought, he said later, was to give the ball as quickly as possible to Aaron, who had gone through so much to hit it and was the only man who deserved to have it.

On September 14, 1996, Mark McGwire, playing for the Oakland Athletics in a game against the Indians at Jacobs Field in Cleveland, hit his 50th home run of the season, the first time he had ever reached such a lofty plateau. The ball was caught by 11-year-old Adam Ulm of North Canton, Ohio, who exchanged it with McGwire for a team ball autographed by all the A's players and another one signed just by Big Mac.

Two years later, on September 8, 1998, the 6-5, 250-pound red-headed and goateed slugger, having subsequently moved over to the Cardinals, achieved an even more personally satisfying (and historic) benchmark when he hit his 62nd home run of the season, breaking Roger Maris's 37-year-old mark. It occurred in the fourth inning against the Cubs, the ball jumping off McGwire's bat on a line and barely clearing the fence in left. The nearly 50,000 people at Busch Stadium rose to their feet as one, and the game stopped for ten minutes in celebration.

One of the few at Busch not in a celebratory mood was Cubs pitcher Steve Trachsel, who gave up the home run. He said later, "Maybe when my career is over I'll think about it. Right now it's just another home run. I've given up a billion of them."

At the time, experts thought No. 62 could be worth $1 million or more. But Tim Forneris, a groundskeeper for the Cardinals who scooped up the ball in an area in front of the left-field stands, decided not to sell it. A sudden celebrity by virtue of his having held, for a time, a baseball treasure in the palm of his hand, he presented the ball to McGwire with the words "I believe I have something that belongs to you."

"Life is all about experiences," Forneris said to the swarm of reporters seeking his comments. "They can't take this away from me. It's better than a million dollars in the bank."

Sammy Sosa, who was in right field for the Cubs when McGwire hit his record-breaker, waited until he returned home to Wrigley Field to hit *his* 60th of the season to tie Ruth's old mark and become the fourth person in major league history to hit 60 or more home runs in a season. With the wind blowing out, Sosa's seventh-inning shot sailed across Waveland Avenue onto the front steps of someone's house.

"We had men on second and third, and I didn't want to strike out," said Sosa, who fouled off a few pitches before connecting. "I came through. I hit 60, I jumped up and said, 'Yes,' and that was about it. I didn't want to show the other team up."

Not so concerned about the social niceties, Cubs fans went nuts, chanting Sammy's name and giving the ebullient, Dominican-born outfielder a raucous standing ovation. Many of them stayed long after the game was over to see him emerge from the dugout for an on-field TV interview, chanting his name in the background while he spoke. "I just have to say that I could never feel more happy than I do today," Sammy told the interviewer.

Having outscrambled a bunch of other ball hogs to put his mitts on No. 60, Chicago resident Herb Neurauter was equally thrilled. Herb gave the ball to Sosa in exchange for some pictures with him and autographed baseballs, including one with the No. 60 next to Sammy's name.

Mark McGwire's 70th came at Busch on the final day of the season. The lucky fan who caught it was a researcher at Washington University in St. Louis named Philip Ozersky, who became an instant millionaire after selling the ball at a famous New York auction in January of the following year. At that auction, Spawn comics creator and toy mogul Todd McFarlane won a bidding contest with another collector over the prized souvenir, paying slightly more than $3 million for the ball, the most expensive single piece of sports memorabilia ever purchased.

Pricey as it was, the McGwire ball was but one of the items in McFarlane's extensive collection, which included Big Mac's 63rd, 67th, 68th, and 69th of '98, plus Sammy's 20th in June of that year (and 33rd overall), which set a record for most home runs in a month, and his 66th and final of the season, for which McFarlane paid a relatively paltry $175,000.

In the euphoria surrounding the '98 season, many observers thought 70 was an unassailable record that would stand for decades. One of these was McFarlane, a Canadian-born resident of Phoenix, who, besides being a huge baseball fan, owns a piece of the Edmonton Oilers hockey club. Then came 2001 and Barry Bonds started hitting . . . and hitting . . . and hitting home runs. When the Giants star reached 63 in early September, McFarlane finally came to accept the bitter truth.

"It was the first time I actually acknowledged it could happen," he recalls. "It was like coldhearted reality set in. 'Oh my gosh, he can actually get this record. What are you going to do now?'"

What all this meant to his $3 million investment was painful to consider: "My ball becomes worth about three dollars and fifty cents, and I become the biggest idiot in the world."

On October 5, 2001, Bonds broke the record with his 71st home run of the season, off Chan Ho Park of the Dodgers at Pacific Bell (now SBC) Park in San Francisco. Jerry Rose, a 49-year-old long-time Giants fan and season-ticket holder, snagged the ball near the 421-foot sign in center field. Security personnel quickly escorted him out of the stands to a private room in the park where Rose, a Yolo County director of employment and social services, reflected on his incredible luck. In all his years of going to games, it was the first ball he had ever caught.

But it also made him very, very nervous. After the game, he went home and had the ball locked in a bank safety-deposit box. But what good is owning a piece of historic memorabilia if you can't actually look at it?

"I talked to my friends about keeping it, but you can't keep that around the house," he was saying. "It's impossible to just stick it on the mantel and enjoy it. In order to do that, I'd have to have a lifetime contract with Brinks."

Rose sold the ball on consignment to Guernsey's in New York, the auction house that had handled the bidding for McGwire's 70th.

Two innings after dishing up No. 71, Park served up another gopher ball to Bonds. No. 72, however, eluded all the people lusting after it, kicking out of the stands and bounding back onto the playing field. Giants center fielder Marquis Grissom picked the ball up and it was later given to the man who hit it.

A strange and twisted fate befell No. 73, Bonds's last, and therefore most valuable, home run of the season. It came on October 7 and landed in the right-field stands at SBC amid a surging, grasping, clawing mass of humanity. Berkeleyite Alex Popov apparently got a glove on it, but in all the pushing and shoving, another man, Patrick Hayashi, ended up with it. The two took their fight over who truly owned the ball to court. In late 2002, after a 14-day trial with 17 witnesses, a San Francisco Superior Court judge ruled that the ball, which had been stored in a bank vault while the dispute was being resolved, should be auctioned off with the two men splitting the proceeds equally.

In June 2003, in an auction hosted by Leland's at Times Square in New York City and televised live across the nation, Bonds's record-setter sold for just over $500,000. Although the purchase price was lower than expected, it was still the third-highest sum ever paid for a baseball, behind only McGwire's 70th and Aaron's 755th (the final home run of Hank's career, which sold for $650,000). The man who bought No. 73 was Todd McFarlane.

In April 2004, Barry Bonds hit his lifetime 660th home run, tying the all-time mark of his godfather longtime family friend Willie Mays. The high, soaring shot cleared the right-field stands and landed in the water at McCovey Cove, the arm of San Francisco Bay that borders the Giants' park.

As is the case at many San Francisco home games, a small flotilla of vessels floated around the cove, their owners waiting for the chance to grab a Bonds home-run souvenir. When No. 660 splashed down, every craft in the water raced frantically for it. But California governor Arnold Schwarzenegger got there first, diving out of his kayak and into the water to retrieve it.

Actually, it wasn't Schwarzenegger; it only was a man wearing a

Schwarzenegger mask. His name was Larry Ellison, and he frequently wears an Arnold mask when paddling around McCovey Cove, hoping to catch balls hit there. Ellison, a Bay Area computer salesman, had netted plenty of batting practice balls in his kayak but never one from a game, and certainly never one as important as No. 660.

Knowing how personally significant it was to Bonds, Ellison traded the ball for some Giants tickets.

A couple of months after Bonds tied, then surpassed, Mays in lifetime home runs, Ken Griffey, Jr., of the Reds established a benchmark of his own, hitting his 500th home run, in a career destined to go through Cooperstown. He knocked it out of the park in Busch Stadium, the site of so many of Mark McGwire's storied home-run balls. Being at a visiting park where the fans might be expected to be less friendly to him, and with collectors saying that No. 500 could be worth as much as $50,000, Griffey never expected to see the ball again after it disappeared into the seats at Busch.

What happened next surprised him. The fan who caught it, a 19-year-old Southern Illinois student named Mark Crummley, gave it to Junior with no strings attached. He didn't want anything for it: no tickets, no autographed balls, no pictures of him posing with the star.

"It's not my ball," Crummley said simply. "It belongs to him."

An astonished yet grateful Griffey responded to this gesture with generosity of his own, giving Crummley (who did not ask for any of this) a jersey he wore the day he hit No. 500, Reds memorabilia, four game tickets, and four round-trip air tickets with accommodations for the All-Star Game in Houston. It was also arranged for Crummley to go on the field with his glove and chase down fly balls during the All-Star home-run-hitting contest.

Spitballers

The first major league game in baseball history took place May 4, 1871, in Fort Wayne, Indiana, between the Fort Wayne Kekiongas and the Forest Citys of Cleveland. The Kekiongas came out on top, 2 to 0, behind the shutout pitching of dark-haired, mustachioed Bobby Mathews. According to those who know such things, Mathews used a spitball, touching his fingers to his lips before he threw each pitch.

Despite the claims about Mathews, many believe that it was a San Francisco–born outfielder, George Hildebrand, who invented the spitball. According to the story, after playing less than a dozen games for Brooklyn in 1902, Hildebrand came back to California and started experimenting with wetting up a baseball with saliva. Watching how the ball moved with spit on it, he showed what he did to a California League pitcher named Elmer Stricklett. Only 5 feet 6 inches tall, 140 pounds, and unable to intimidate batters with his fastball, Elmer relied on craft and guile to succeed as a pitcher. This made him open to the idea of learning how to throw a wet one, and Stricklett became one of the earliest spitballers in the big leagues.

Bugs Raymond pitched for the New York Giants in the early years of the 1900s, and "what a terrific spitball pitcher he was," recalled teammate and fellow pitcher Rube Marquard. "Bugs drank a lot, you know, and sometimes it seemed like the more he drank, the better he pitched. They used to say he didn't spit on the ball; he blew his breath on it, and the ball would come up drunk."

One time Bugs was having lunch at a restaurant when a waiter asked him to demonstrate his spitter. Unhappy that his meal had been interrupted, he licked his fingers, grabbed a glass on the table, and threw the glass through the front window.

"That's how it's done," Bugs said. "See the break?"

In 1920, the major leagues banned the spitball, greaseball, jellyball, scuffball, and other illegal pitches, but allowed the men who threw these pitches before this date to continue throwing them until their careers ended. The last man to throw a legal spitter in the majors was that old gamer Burleigh Grimes, the Brooklyn Dodgers right-hander who retired his spittoon once and for all in 1934.

But pitchers kept wetting baseballs and scuffing them up, even though the practice was illegal. Many needed to do it in order to make a living in the game. The story is told about the manager who came out to the mound to talk to his young pitcher who was getting roughed up by the opposition.

"Son," he said. "Are you cheating?"

"Nah," said the pitcher.

"Well," said the manager, "it's about time you start."

"A guy who cheats in a friendly game of cards is a cheater," George Bamberger used to say. "A guy who throws a spitball to support his family is a competitor."

Lew Burdette, a pitcher for the Braves and other teams in the '50s and '60s, was a competitor. He threw a spitter that made another tough competitor, Richie Ashburn, hopping mad. His veins bulging on his neck, Richie would yell at the umpire for allowing Burdette to cheat and then at Burdette for doing the cheating.

A hard-boiled West Virginian who won three games, including two shutouts, for the Braves in their 1957 World Series championship, Burdette refused to take any guff from Ashburn, yelling back at him, "You keep yelling about it and I'll keep throwing it."

★   ★   ★

Whitey Ford was well known for his habit of doctoring baseballs, especially late in his career. He sometimes applied a sticky substance to his left hand to get a better grip on the ball. This substance he hid in a deodorant can in which he had cut out the bottom, applying it much like a roll-on deodorant.

Wanting to play a trick on Yogi Berra, Mickey Mantle took Whitey's fake deodorant can and put it next to Yogi's locker. Without paying much attention to what he was doing, Yogi grabbed the can and went for a shower. After he was done, he applied Whitey's stickum substance to his armpits. A moment later, in a total panic, he came running out of the shower screaming about his arms being glued to his sides.

The Yankees trainer first applied rubbing alcohol to Yogi's underarms. When that didn't work, he snipped away some of his armpit hair. This finally succeeded in freeing Yogi's arms.

Because of the illegal nature of their activities, spitballers do not tend to tell other people, even their own teammates, what they are doing. Reds pitcher Bob Purkey told only his catcher. The joke was that nobody in baseball realized Purkey threw a spitter until one day his catcher appeared behind the plate wearing a bib.

The best-known and most successful spitballer of the modern era was Gaylord Perry, who pitched for the Giants, Indians, Padres, and other teams in a 22-season Hall of Fame career. After he hit a home run off Perry in an All-Star Game, reporters asked Hank Aaron what pitch he had hit.

"A spitball," said Hank, "down and in."

Among the substances used by Perry were Vaseline and lubricating jelly, which, when rubbed on a baseball, make it do things in the air it does not ordinarily do. These substances also smell, which was why rival manager Billy Martin once supposedly brought a blood-hound to the park to smell Perry's gym bag. "The dog died of a heart attack," said Martin.

It should be noted that many people suspected Billy and his longtime pitching coach, Art Fowler, of teaching their pitchers how to throw spitters, and that much of the success the Oakland A's had in their starting rotation in the early 1980s was due to the pitch.

Gaylord Perry also offered instruction on how to do it, but it came with a price. "When Gaylord and I were teammates," remembers Steve Stone, "he offered to show me the whole course. But he said, 'It'll cost you three thousand dollars.' "

Stone, who won 25 games for the Orioles and later became a broadcaster, declined the offer.

One reason spitball throwers are successful is that they can deke out batters. A hitter may think a spitter is coming, even if it is not, which allows the man on the mound to slip a different pitch past him.

Gaylord Perry was a master at this sort of deception. His throwing hand would move constantly before each pitch, touching the bill of his cap, behind his ear, his neck, his belt, his arms, across his jersey, back to his cap—all with the idea of making the hitter think that the ball was being slathered with Vaseline or some other greasy substance.

Watching Perry's routine from an opposing dugout, George Bamberger wasn't fooled, though. "I don't think any are decoys," he said. "I think he's got that stuff everyplace."

Bamberger himself threw a spitter when he was in the minors, naming the pitch in honor of his birthplace: "The Staten Island sinker."

After he became a coach for the Orioles, he taught the pitch to left-hander Ross "Scuzz" Grimsley, who, said *Washington Post* columnist Tom Boswell, had "enough greasy kid stuff in his ultralong curly hair to give A. J. Foyt a lube job and oil change." Despite complaints about him from hitters and opposing managers, umpires never liked to check to see if Scuzz was throwing a spitball because they didn't want to put their fingers in his hair.

Yet another who apparently used the spitter (it's pretty much out of date now; hardly anyone throws it) was Don Sutton of the Dodgers. Sutton had a sense of humor about it, hiding notes around his uniform for when the umpires came out to inspect him for Vaseline or perhaps a piece of sandpaper that he may have cut the ball with.

When the ump looked in his pocket, one note said, "Not here." When the ump searched his belt, another note said, "You're getting warmer." The umps never did catch Sutton, who won 324 games and, like Perry, is now in the Hall of Fame.

Dick Stuart

Dick Stuart's breakout year came in 1956, when he hit 66 home runs and had 158 runs batted in for the Lincoln Chiefs of Lincoln, Nebraska. Granted, these prodigious totals occurred in the Class A Western League, but the 23-year-old Stuart, who was as big (6-foot-4) as he was strong, appeared to have the power and swagger needed to become a big-time major league slugger.

"I just want to walk down the street and hear them say, 'Jesus, there goes Dick Stuart!'" he told a reporter, echoing a famous line by Ted Williams. "I like to see my name in the paper, especially the headlines. I crave it. I deserve them headlines."

★   ★   ★

Of course, there was this little problem. This was in the years before the designated hitter rule, and every regular who came up to bat was also required to play the field. This proved to be a daunting challenge for Stuart, who was an awful, awful fielder.

Pittsburgh Pirates manager Bobby Bragan said as much when he got his first look at Dick at spring training the year after his big season in Lincoln, declaring him "one of the worst outfielders I've ever seen." The Pirates switched the right-handed slugger to first base, figuring he could get into less trouble with his glove there. They were wrong.

Stuart played part-time first base for Pittsburgh in '58, establishing himself early on as a man to be feared with a glove on his hand. In one game, he made three errors on three consecutive ground balls. On the fourth grounder hit to him, he snagged the ball perfectly and ran toward first base while waving away the pitcher coming over to cover the bag.

But as he was waving, the ball flew out of his glove and bounced down the right-field line as the batter rounded first and kept going. "We'd have had the guy at third," said Gene Freese, who was playing third base for the Pirates that day. "But I was laughing too hard."

"I know I'm the world's worst fielder," said Stuart, "but who gets paid for fielding? There isn't a great fielder in baseball getting the kind of dough I get for hitting."

Stuart was right. It was his bat, not his glove, that kept him in the bigs—27 taters in 1959, his first full season in the majors, and 23 the next year. In 1961, his best season as a hitter, his numbers were nothing to laugh at: .301 batting average, 35 home runs, 117 RBIs. Pie Traynor, the Hall of Fame third baseman who played 17 seasons in Pittsburgh in the '20s and '30s, said that one of Stuart's home runs at Forbes Field, the Pirates' home park for many years, was the longest he'd ever seen hit there.

Like many a ballplayer, Stuart did not lack for ego. When he signed autographs, he often included "66" as part of his name, a nod to his 66-home-run season as a minor leaguer. A sharp dresser, he was a bit of a dandy who liked looking good, off the field and on. Looking sharp in his uni, he said, even made him hit better.

"I add 20 points to my average if I know I look bitchin' out there," he said.

Nothing Stuart did, however, could make him field better. "Everybody liked Dick," said a teammate on the Pirates, Dick Schofield, "but he did have trouble with that leather thing."

Before the start of a game, the Forbes Field public address announcer addressed the fans, saying over the loudspeakers, "Anyone who interferes with the ball in play will be ejected from the ballpark."

Sitting in the Pittsburgh dugout, manager Danny Murtaugh leaned over to a coach and said, "I hope Stuart doesn't think that means him."

The team bus was passing by a concrete mixing plant in Pittsburgh when a Pirates player yelled out, "Stop the bus! Stuart needs a new glove!"

After being hit by a pitch in a game, Stuart staggered toward first base. The Pittsburgh trainer ran onto the field and asked him if he felt dizzy.

"No more than usual," he replied.

Stuart was aware of his liabilities as fielder—"One night in Pittsburgh," he joked, "30,000 fans gave me a standing ovation when I caught a hot-dog wrapper on the fly"—and so was everyone else. "He's a Williams-type player," a reporter said about him. "Hits like

Ted and fields like Esther." It was said that Stuart practiced only healthy habits. He didn't drink or smoke or stay out late, and he always made sure to stay out of the way of hard-hit ground balls.

Eventually, Pittsburgh gave up on him and traded him to Boston. The Red Sox liked the idea of the big righty swinging for the short left-field fence at Fenway Park, but unfortunately for them, Stuart had to play the field too.

His nicknames were Dr. Strangeglove, Stonefingers, the Boston Strangler, Clank (for the sound the ball made when it hit his glove), and the Ancient Mariner (because "he stoppeth one in three"). One of his new Red Sox teammates, referring to the official scorer's designation for an error by the first baseman, joked that the license plates for Stuart's car should read "E-3."

But the man could hit. Give him that—he could hit. In 1963, Stonefingers clubbed 42 home runs and an American League–leading 118 RBIs to earn the Comeback Player of the Year Award.

The following year, a cop pulled him over on a Boston street for driving without a current registration sticker on his license plate. When asked by the officer why he still had the 1963 registration, Stuart said, "I had such a good year, I didn't want to forget it."

Stuart became a crowd favorite in Boston before being traded away. He bounced around a few teams in the United States before going to Japan and playing on a professional team there. "After being the only American player on a team in Hiroshima," he said, "nothing bothers me anymore." He returned to the States, hit a homer for the '69 Angels, and hung up his glove with a clang.

Stunts

In the middle years of the nineteenth century, the United States decided to honor its first president with a monument in keeping with his great character and enormous contributions to the founding of the republic. The monument, designed by architect Robert Mills, was in the form of an obelisk, a shaft or column with a pyramid at the top. With an interior composed of granite, an exterior of white marble, the first cornerstone of the obelisk was set into place in 1848.

The masonry structure rose to a height of about 150 feet until, in the mid-1850s, the builders ran out of money and construction ceased. One year led to the next and the building remained unfinished for more than 20 years. It was not until 1878 that the Congress appropriated funds to resume construction and finish the job. The 555-foot-high Washington Monument was finally dedicated in 1885.

Almost immediately after its completion, people began to wonder what would happen if someone dropped a baseball from the top of the monument. Could another person waiting on the ground catch it? It was only a matter of time before someone tried to do it.

The late baseball historian Lee Allen gives credit to a man named H. P. Burney for actively promoting the idea of the Washington Monument ball drop. Burney worked as a clerk at the Arlington Hotel in Washington, which joined the National League the year after the monument was opened to the public. Visiting teams often stayed at the Arlington, and Burney discussed his pet idea with ballplayers and anyone else who was interested.

Apparently, several players of this era, including Buck Ewing, a highly regarded mustachioed catcher and first baseman, took the dare. They tried and failed to catch a ball launched from the top of the monument, which must have convinced Burney that it was impossible to perform the feat, because in August 1894, he argued strongly with Chicago player-manager Cap Anson that it could not be done. Anson disagreed just as strongly, and as two men often do when they disagree on something, they placed a wager to see who was right.

The task of catching the ball fell not to Anson but to one of his players, Pop Schriver, a catcher. Clark Griffith, then a pitcher who years later came to own the Washington franchise, climbed to the top of the monument while Schriver, Burney, Anson, and some others with a betting interest waited below. All this had to be done on the sly, because monument officials discouraged such stunts.

Griffith stood at the north window just below the base of the pyramid, which extended upward another fifty feet. This made the height of the drop about 505 feet.

It is not clear if he dropped or tossed the ball. In any case, the first ball was a test to see what would happen when it hit the ground. It bounced, but only a little, which made Schriver think he could handle the next one. He stepped up, the ball came down, and he snagged it in his glove. A police officer then appeared, telling everyone to leave.

The most famous ball-catching stunt in Washington Monument history occurred on August 21, 1908, and it also came about because of a bet.

One account says the wager was between two sportswriters. Another claims it was between a sportswriter and Washington catcher Gabby Street. It is possible that a whole number of people had money riding on whether or not the chatty and amiable Street, whose real name was Charles and who was known as the favorite catcher of hard-throwing Washington right-hander Walter Johnson, could make the grab.

The naysayers, those who bet against Gabby, looked in good shape during the early rounds. With a strong breeze making it hard to judge the ball's flight, he missed on 12 consecutive tries.

But, on his lucky thirteenth, Gabby hauled one in, reportedly winning $500 for his efforts. That afternoon, he played for Washington in a game.

Gabby's feat made news around the country. One San Francisco newspaper described it as "unprecedented." In making the catch, Gabby had used a catcher's glove manufactured by a sporting goods firm, A. J. Reach Company, which placed a full-page advertisement in its well-read annual baseball publication, trumpeting the event and claiming it had never been done before. The ad also noted that not one of the dozen Reach-made balls missed by Street that hit the pavement received any permanent damage, attesting to the quality of its products.

Lost in the hubbub was Pop Schriver's earlier achievement, and Gabby Street became widely but incorrectly known as the first man to catch a ball from the top of the Washington Monument.

In the years to come, others followed in the path forged by Schriver and Street. In 1911, Billy Sullivan, a catcher with the White Sox, decided to conduct an experiment. Wondering if it was easier to catch a ball that was dropped or thrown from the monument, Sullivan first tried his luck with a dropped ball. It took three or four tries before he caught one. Then he stepped away from the base of the column and received a thrown ball from the man at the top. A thrown ball, Billy concluded, was much easier because he could better judge the arc of the ball's flight rather than one that was just falling straight down.

★   ★   ★

With all the publicity about Washington Monument ball catches, other players in other cities naturally sought to duplicate or surpass these stunts in order to claim the distinction of being the man who had caught a baseball dropped from the highest height ever. One afternoon at spring training camp at Daytona Beach, Florida, Brooklyn manager Wilbert Robinson and some of his Dodgers spotted an airplane overhead and wondered if it would be possible to catch a baseball dropped from it.

They subsequently sought out the pilot, who was agreeable to the idea of letting the team's trainer accompany her into the plane and drop a ball out of it. All the Dodgers, including Robinson, a pleasant, kindly former catcher in his first year of managing the team, took their places on the practice field, looking skyward. All were supposed to try to catch the ball, not knowing that one member of the team, the impish Casey Stengel, secretly substituted the ball for a grapefruit and prevailed upon the trainer to drop it instead. The trainer went along with the prank and let the grapefruit fly, and— well, let's let Casey take it from here:

"Robbie saw it coming and waved everybody away like an outfielder and said, 'I've got it, I've got it.' And the thing kept coming closer and getting bigger. He got under this grapefruit, thinking it was a baseball, which hit him right on this pitcher's glove he put on, and you know, the insides of it flew all over, seeds on his face and uniform, and flipped him back right over on his back. He lay there, looking like a ghost. Everybody came running up and everybody commenced laughing, all except Robbie, who got burned up."

Dazed and staggering from the blow, Wilbert at first thought the grapefruit juice was his own blood, only gradually realizing that he had been made the butt of a practical joke. The prankster Stengel stayed with Brooklyn for a few more seasons, but not the trainer. He was soon looking for a new job.

"The greatest of all stunt catches," according to *Baseball Digest,* occurred on an August day in 1939 when a minor league catcher named Joe Sprinz attempted to snag a ball dropped from a Goodyear blimp flying 800 feet above Treasure Island in San Francisco Bay. The stunt, which took place as part of the World's Fair being held that year in San Francisco, attracted 1,500 onlookers curious to see if Sprinz could break the world record set the previous year when Indians catcher Frankie Pytlak (and possibly Hank Helf, too) caught a ball dropped from Cleveland's Terminal Tower at a height of about 700 feet.

Sprinz, who had caught five balls dropped from the top of a 437-foot building earlier in the year, watched as the first ball dropped from the blimp known as *Volunteer* landed hard, very hard, in an empty bleachers area. The ball's falling speed—estimated to be 145 mph, or 17 feet per second—shocked him, as did the force with which it struck the wooden stands. He could get killed, he realized, if he misjudged a ball coming down that fast.

But Sprinz, whose nickname was Mule, grew up in south St. Louis, and as he said once, "They called you chicken there if you backed down on something." The Mule was no chicken, and after four missed attempts he was determined to get a glove on the fifth ball that came hurtling down out of the cloudless coastal sky.

Coincidentally, Sprinz, a native San Franciscan, was celebrating his 37th birthday that day. He had played a little in the majors earlier in the decade but had spent most of his career with the hometown San Francisco Seals of the Pacific Coast League. Dressed in a Seals uniform, he wore a cap but no sunglasses and no dried mud under his eyes, which players in that era used to decrease the sun's glare.

Looking straight up into the afternoon sun, Sprinz never knew what hit him. Trying to catch the ball not with his glove stretched out in front of him away from his body, but rather raised high near his face as if he were trying to grab a high pop fly, it hit his face like a hammer. As the ball bounced away, Sprinz staggered forward a few steps, burying his face in his hands before collapsing to the ground.

People rushed to his aid and he never lost consciousness as he was rushed to the hospital, where he remained for the next three months. Although his jaw was not broken as first feared, he lost five teeth and suffered a dozen pencil-line cracks in his cheekbone. Doctors installed a bridge for his upper teeth, and he suffered splitting headaches for years after the incident.

A professor at the University of California at Berkeley calculated that the ball struck him with the impact of 8,050 foot-pounds. Sprinz, no mathematician, said it felt like the blimp, not a ball, fell on him. Forced to miss the remainder of the Coast League season, he came back the next year and caught 129 games for the Seals. For his efforts, Sprinz earned a mention in the *Guinness Book of World Records* for "Highest Catch Attempt."

One would think the Sprinz disaster would have put an end to such ball-catching stunts, but this was not the case. In the late 1950s, Dutch Dotterer, a catcher with the Reds, spoke three languages and had a master's degree from Syracuse. Bright as he was, he still agreed to try to catch a ball dropped from a helicopter hovering above Cincinnati's Crosley Field at about 575 feet. Dutch managed to make the grab safely.

The frequently traded, frequently released Kurt Bevacqua played for an assortment of teams in his 15-year big league career. A sign above his clubhouse locker read, "If I hang around here another 20 years, maybe I'll get my act together."

A hustling, energetic utility man, he understood his role in baseball: "You're a Lloyds of London policy for a period of time, then you're gone." He played anywhere his manager asked him to—outfield, infield, catcher—and in 1982 the San Diego Padres asked him to participate in a ball-catching stunt to raise money for charity. The ever-willing Bevacqua, who had once won a TV bubble-gum-blowing contest, said yes.

The balls were tossed from the top of the 325-foot-high Imperial

Tower building in downtown San Diego, and Bevacqua caught five of them. His greatest moment in baseball, however, came two years later when he hit a three-run homer to help the Padres beat the Tigers in Game 2 of the 1984 World Series, San Diego's only win of the Series.

Trades

After the 1947 season, Bill Veeck, owner of the Cleveland Indians, seriously considered trading his All-Star shortstop, Lou Boudreau. The Indians had finished in the middle of the pack and Veeck felt that Boudreau, who also managed the club, would be good trade bait to acquire some other players who might help the team more. But hearing about a possible deal to get rid of their popular player-manager, Indians fans protested the move, and Veeck never went ahead with it. Boudreau stayed put.

The next season, Boudreau hit .355 with 106 runs batted in and won American League MVP honors while managing Cleveland to the pennant and a World Series championship.

"Sometimes," said Veeck philosophically, "the best trades are the ones you don't make."

Casey Stengel was managing the Yankees and Bob Cerv was playing part-time outfield for the club when the two of them were seated next to each other one day in the Yankees' dugout.

Neither said a word to the other until Stengel broke the long silence.

"Nobody knows this," he said, leaning over to Cerv, "but one of us has just been traded to Kansas City."

After grabbing Rookie of the Year honors for the Reds in 1956, Frank Robinson hit .323 with 124 runs batted in and 37 home runs in Cincinnati's pennant-winning year of 1961. The next year, he topped those numbers in each category: .342, 39, 136.

But by the end of the '65 season his production had fallen off some, and Reds general manager William DeWitt traded his star outfielder to the Orioles. Asked to explain the reason for the move, DeWitt cited Robinson's age, saying, "He's an *old* 30."

The next season, the elderly Robinson won the Triple Crown— .316 average, 49 home runs, 122 runs batted in—and led Baltimore to a World Series title. In six seasons with the O's, he played on four pennant-winners and two world champions. The Reds fired DeWitt.

In the middle 1970s, the Yankees and Pirates swapped pitchers: Dock Ellis coming over to New York from Pittsburgh and Doc Medich leaving New York for the Bucs.

In 1976, Dock Ellis won 17 games for the pennant-winning Yankees while Doc Medich, who earned his nickname because he was then studying medicine, had a losing record as the Pirates finished out of the running in the National League East.

Assessing the relative merits of the trade, Pittsburgh sportswriter Charles Feeney said, "Ellis is probably a better doctor too."

In his first season in the big leagues, Jose Gonzalez played shortstop for a few games for the St. Louis Cardinals. The next year, when he came to San Francisco in a trade, he asked people to call him by a new name: Uribe Gonzalez.

Then Jose, er Uribe, changed his mind once more, deciding to be called by the name he came to be known by in the majors: Jose Uribe.

Observing all these changes, Giants coach Rocky Bridges remarked, "Jose truly was the player to be named later in the trade."

Bobby Valentine

Was there a better player in Connecticut prep football history than Bobby Valentine? Nearly 40 years after his last game for Rippowam High, some Stamford old-timers still think the cocky kid who scored more than 50 career touchdowns was the best. No Connecticut high school football player has ever won All-American honors three years in a row, the way Bobby did.

Bobby could play baseball, too, and after turning down a bunch of college football scholarship offers, the 18-year-old signed with the Los Angeles Dodgers organization. His first minor league team was in Ogden, and his manager there was Tommy Lasorda, then working his way up the Dodgers hierarchy. Lasorda and Valentine hit it off partly because the youngster was such a good player and partly because his personality—self-confidence, one might say, bordering on arrogance—did not bother the older man.

"He was insufferable," Lasorda said, remembering the young Valentine, "but in a good way."

Valentine went on to become Pacific Coast League Player of the Year and made the big leagues in '71, but a series of injuries steadily reduced his effectiveness and he never became the star many thought he'd be. Finished as a player before his 30th birthday, he coached for the Mets before taking over as manager of the Rangers in 1985. Although leading Texas to some winning seasons, he never produced a division title and after eight years got his pink slip. Then came a year at the Mets' Triple A farm team in Norfolk, after which his managing career took a most unusual turn. Hired by the Chiba Lotte Marines, Bobby Valentine became the first American to ever manage a Japanese professional baseball team.

★　★　★

Valentine knew he had arrived in a different land when the Chiba Lotte owner decided to show him the correct way to hit a baseball by taking up a samurai sword in both hands and chopping bamboo.

Some of the Chiba Lotte players distrusted Valentine at first because he was an American. To win them over, he engaged in a ritual of Japanese baseball: fielding ground balls. Not just a few ground balls for a little while, but hundreds and hundreds of them hit to him over the course of nearly four hours. By the time he was done, he had earned the respect of his players.

No matter where he goes, no matter what he does, Bobby is Bobby—insufferable, but in a good way—and Bobby was definitely himself while in Japan. Often seen in public, mixing with fans at sushi restaurants, riding his bicycle around town, signing autographs, posing for pictures, he became a popular personality in the country.

He was not so popular with Japanese baseball traditionalists, however, as he cut back on the amount of time his players hit batting practice—the norm was four hours per session—and reduced the workload for his starting pitchers. Starting pitchers in Japan are still expected to go the full nine innings, but Valentine instituted a pitch count that restricted the number of pitches they could throw. Then he pulled them from the game if they exceeded it, even if they reached this number before the ninth.

Valentine's ways were described as *chigaimasu,* which in Japanese means "change," "different," or "incorrect." The American's changes were too different for Chiba Lotte's samurai-toting owner, and after a year with the club, he left Japan and returned home to assume his old post in Norfolk with the Mets. After the parent club got rid of Dallas Green as manager, it looked within its own system and tabbed the much-traveled but still supremely confident Valentine.

★ ★ ★

In perhaps a reflection of his experience in Japanese baseball, with its emphasis on discipline, Bobby arrived at his first spring training camp for the Mets having planned out the schedule for all 45 days of practice. Unsure at first but willing to try anything if it helped them win, the players quickly caught on to their new manager's enthusiasm and clear knowledge of the game.

Some Mets got together and presented him with a huge cake that said, "Happy Valentine's Day." Then they smashed the cake in Valentine's face.

"Another rule," said Valentine, wiping the icing away with a towel. "No cake in the face."

It became a pregame ritual with the Mets, who began to win under Valentine's leadership. After the playing of the national anthem, Bobby would say, "Hey, this is a really big game." And a player would ask, "Why's that?" And Bobby would answer, "Because it's the one we're playing."

Al Leiter was pitching for the Marlins against the Mets at Pro Player Stadium when he heard somebody yakking at him from the visitors' bench. "This guy ain't nothin'," said the squeaky, high-pitched voice. "He ain't gonna make it past the fifth inning. . . ."

Leiter did not want to look directly into the dugout, because that would have indicated he heard what was being said, and that it was possibly rattling him. But the razzing continued and the left-hander kept listening to see if he could pick out its source. Because if it had been a player talking all that trash, the next time he came up to bat, as Leiter said, "I would have stuck one in his ear."

Gradually, Leiter figured out that the squeaky, high-pitched rattle belonged not to a player but to Valentine. Bobby's bench jockeying had little effect, though. Florida won the game, Leiter pitched well, and afterward he told the press, "I want to thank the Mets manager for firing me up."

The next year, Leiter came over to the Mets and got to know Valentine and grew to like him, even though, as Leiter says, Bobby is "perceived as a guy who doesn't listen to others and is kind of a know-it-all, and he rubs people the wrong way."

One Met he rubbed the wrong way was Todd Hundley, who was coming off a 41-homer season when Valentine joined the club. But Bobby thought he could get more out of his catcher, criticizing his off-field habits to the press: "I think he doesn't sleep enough. He's a nocturnal person. He has a real hard time getting to sleep after games. I think he needs to change his ways."

Hundley was aghast. "Did I get arrested at four in the morning?" he said to reporters who asked him about Valentine's remarks. "Did someone in a bar say I was out all night? What did I do? I didn't do anything." Todd added, referring to his skipper, "I don't get paid enough to be friends with that guy."

Hundley and his manager never did get to be chummy, and a couple of months into the '98 season, the Mets traded for Mike Piazza, an unmistakable sign that Todd's time in New York was just about over. By the following season, he was wearing Dodger blue.

Valentine was known as "Top Step Bobby" for his habit of standing on the top dugout step during a game, intently watching the proceedings on the field and chattering away. Against Toronto he got into a big argument with an umpire, who tossed him from the game. But Top Step Bobby reappeared in the 12th inning wearing sunglasses and a fake mustache. The commissioner's office didn't appreciate the joke and fined him for returning to a game in which he'd been ejected.

During his often-turbulent reign in New York, the *Sporting News* called him "the most hated man in baseball," after which Bobby began introducing himself to people this way: "Hi, I'm the most hated man in baseball."

Al Leiter talks about going to a party held one year before the *Sports Illustrated* Sportsman of the Year banquet in New York and feeling intimidated by all the celebrities present. He was standing around the edges of the crowd, not mingling with anybody, when that familiar squeaky voice rang out, "Al, get over here!"

Al walked over and there was Bobby, chatting up Donald Trump. Recalls Leiter, "I came over and he said, 'Meet Donald.' And Donald Trump turned around. Bobby was palling around with him, patting him, doing the political grab-ass. He feels comfortable with all that."

After being bounced out of New York and deciding, in 2004, to return to Japan to manage the Marines of Chiba Lotte, Bobby was talking about what he liked so much about Japanese baseball and what he didn't like about the American brand.

"It became 'Our stars are going to beat their stars,' " he was saying. "What is that about? I don't get it, and I don't like it. When you start renting stars, and they already have their contracts and their glory, there's no reason to expect them to give their time and effort."

In Japan, by contrast, he said, "I kind of like that I can tell a guy to hit ten straight balls into right field in batting practice, and if he doesn't, he comes over to me afterward and apologizes. I like that."

"I don't have visions of grandeur," Bobby was telling a visitor from America one night while they were having dinner at a restaurant in Kobe. When the visitor gave him a look as if to say, "Bobby Valentine? Not have visions of grandeur?" Bobby added, "Okay, I have visions of small grandeur."

TV's Bryant Gumbel asked Valentine if his translator changes what he says to make it less controversial for Japanese fans.

"No, it's not his job," Bobby said with a smile that seemed to indicate that after all these years he has achieved a degree of self-awareness. "My mouth is plenty big for both my feet."

Earl Weaver

Earl Weaver learned his most lasting baseball lesson on his first day of managing in the Class D minor leagues.

"You've got a hundred more young kids than you have a place for on your club," he was saying, recalling those days. "Every one of 'em has had a goin'-away party. They've kissed everybody and said, 'See you in the majors in two years.' You see these poor kids that shouldn't even be there in the first place. You write on the report card '4-4-4 and out.' That's the lowest rating in everything. Then you call 'em in and say, 'It's the consensus among us that we're going to let you go back home.'

"Some of 'em cry. Some get mad. But none of 'em will leave until you answer one question: 'Skipper, what do *you* think?' And you gotta look every one of those kids in the eye and kick their dreams in the ass and say, 'Kid, there's no way you can make my ball club.'

"They don't have what it takes to make the majors," Weaver concluded sadly. "Just like I never had it."

Weaver never played in the majors, spending twenty seasons in the minors—playing, coaching, managing—before getting his big break with the Baltimore Orioles in 1968. To be a baseball manager, to kick a kid's dream in the ass, he says, you have to be "a rotten bastard. Or, in my case, a little bastard."

Some of the Orioles who played for him would probably agree with that assessment. (Certainly, the umpires would.) But Earl accepted it as a cost of doing business: "To keep your job, you fire others or bench 'em or trade 'em. You're the one who tells them the worst news in their life. You have to do the thinking for 25 guys, and you can't be too close to any of them."

Sportswriter Thomas Boswell, who covered Earl in Baltimore, described him as a "leather-skinned rock." In his late thirties when he joined the O's, he stayed long enough with the club for his hair to turn gray. Short, stocky, blunt-spoken, intensively competitive, and quick to anger, he wanted to win more than anything else.

"On my tombstone just write, 'The sorest loser that ever lived,'" he said once.

The sorest loser that ever lived could also be very funny, sometimes at the expense of those players he refused to get too close to because it might affect how he did his job. Although he won 24 games for Weaver during the O's' 1971 world championship season, Cuban-born left-hander Mike Cuellar struggled late in his career, at one point getting knocked out of the box 13 straight times.

Asked if he planned to give Cuellar any more chances as a starter, Earl replied, "I've given Mike more chances than my first wife."

Pat Kelly played outfield for the Orioles in the late '70s and early '80s and was a devout Christian. He once asked Earl when was the last time he had read the Bible.

"At my father's funeral," said Earl.

"And when was the last time you were on your knees praying?"

"The last time I sent you up to pinch-hit," said Earl.

Another time, Kelly told Weaver, "You've got to walk with the Lord, Skip."

"Kell," said Weaver, "I'd rather you walk with the bases loaded."

Earl explained his philosophy of religion and baseball thusly: "Kell told me one time after he hit a home run that the Lord was looking out for him. I said yeah, and what about that poor guy on the mound who threw you the high slider? We better not be counting on God. I ain't got no stats on God."

One time another Christian on the team, Al Bumbry, who was in a bad hitting slump, told Earl he was going to chapel services to pray.

"Take your bat with you," Earl told him.

Earl smoked cigarettes. Raleighs, to be exact. He joked darkly that he smoked that brand "because with 50,000 coupons they give you a brass coffin." He also gave one of his relievers, Don Stanhouse, the nickname of "Full Pack." The reason? "That's how many cigarettes I smoke when he's on the mound," explained Earl.

Another pitcher who made Earl light up was Ross Grimsley, who had a winning record with the O's in the mid-'80s. Nevertheless, he was getting pounded one day when his manager jogged out to the mound to give him a pep talk.

"If you know how to cheat," Earl told him, recycling an old baseball line, "start now."

Earl Weaver believed in the long ball—"Dr. Longball," he called it, or "The Big Bang Theory." The Big Bang Theory was exquisitely simple: Play for the big inning. Get men on base and have someone hit 'em in with a big home run. "One swing, then trot," as Earl succinctly put it.

Weaver hated to give away an out to the opposing team by bunting along a runner. For him a walk was truly as good as a hit because it put a man on base, a man who would score if the next man up hit it out of the park. The secret of success in managing, he said, was to "get the man up there you want."

He mocked the idea that managers and managerial strategies won ballgames: "The guy who says, 'I love the challenge of managing,' is one step from being out of a job. I don't welcome any challenge. I'd rather have nine guys named Robinson."

Players won ballgames, he said, players who were often acquired during the winter before the games began in earnest. "Smart managing is dumb," he liked to say. "The three-run home run you trade for in the winter will always beat brains."

"My best game plan," he said, "is to sit on the bench and call out specific instructions, like 'C'mon, Boog,' 'Get hold of one, Frank,' 'Let's go, Brooks.'" Power-hitting first baseman Boog Powell, outfielder Frank Robinson, and third baseman Brooks Robinson all contributed greatly to Baltimore's string of division titles and pennants in the late 1960s and '70s. The two Robinsons are in the Hall of Fame.

One time an Oriole hit into a double play with the bases loaded, ending the inning and killing a rally. "You dumb bastard," Weaver said to him when he returned to the dugout. "Haven't you ever heard of a strikeout?"

Weaver did not get along with umpires, and vice versa. Umpires considered him a pest or worse, and he complained about them constantly. Umps tossed him from nearly 100 major league games—one time, it is said, for both games of a doubleheader. Earl got thrown out of one game before the first pitch. He said something an ump didn't like, during the exchange of lineup cards at home plate, and the ump tossed him.

To express his unhappiness with the decisions made by umpires, Weaver tossed bats and gear, threw and kicked his cap, covered home plate with dirt with his spikes. One time he faked a heart attack. Sometimes he used these outbursts as a means of firing up his players or shifting attention away from them so as to relieve them of the pressure they were feeling. Other times he was just plain mad. Turning his O's cap around on his head, his hands on his waist, his stout chest thrust forward, he would stick his face in the face of the umpire, who would sometimes turn his own cap around on his head in order to go nose-to-nose with Earl. Another favorite technique of Earl's was to jab his index finger at the ump while yelling at him.

He got so mad during one game that he uprooted second base from the ground and refused to give it back to the umpires after they tossed him. In the midst of a heated argument with umpire Steve Palermo, he jabbed his finger at him while standing on second base.

Said Palermo afterward, "Earl figured that was the only way he could be as tall as we are, but they don't make bags that tall."

Apart from umpires, Earl's greatest nemesis was one of his own players, Jim Palmer. Well, nemesis is too strong of a term and not exactly correct. Earl loved Jim, because with the tall, handsome, intelligent, strong-jawed right-hander on the mound (Palmer looked good enough to be an underwear model, which, in fact, he was), the O's had an excellent shot at winning every game he pitched.

Still, the two bickered frequently. "Palmer and Weaver were two of the sharpest baseball minds I've ever been around, and each thought he understood the game better than the other," says Brooks Robinson. Mark Belanger, who played shortstop next to Robinson during those years, put it another way: "Palmer airs his opinions on lots of things, and Earl will tell you any damn thing he wants to."

One of the things they quarreled about was the positioning of the outfielders behind Palmer when he pitched. Depending on who was up at the plate, Earl would station the fielders in certain places. Palmer would then take a look at what Earl had done and motion for the outfielders to move a few steps to their left or right.

Weaver finally figured out how to outfox his pitcher, deliberately moving the fielders too far to their left or right, knowing that Palmer would then move them back a few steps. They would then be where Earl wanted them.

One year a sportswriter quoted Palmer as calling Red Sox manager Darrell Johnson "an idiot" for not picking him to be on the American League All-Star team. Palmer denied ever saying this.

"I did not call Johnson an idiot," Palmer said. "Someone else did and I just agreed."

Palmer never called Earl Weaver an idiot, although he did say that "the only thing Weaver knows about a curveball is that he couldn't hit one." He also said, "Instead of having my parents scream at me, now I have Earl Weaver." Weaver himself said he had more fights with Palmer than he did with his wife.

Another thing the two battled about was Palmer's injuries, or lack thereof. To hear Earl tell it, his three-time Cy Young–winning pitcher was the biggest hypochondriac who ever lived:

"The Chinese tell time by the Year of the Horse or the Year of the Dragon. I tell time by the Year of the Back, the Year of the Elbow. Every time Palmer reads about a new ailment, he seems to get it. This year it's the Year of the Ulnar Nerve."

After hearing that Wayne Garland of the Indians had torn the rotator cuff in his pitching shoulder, Palmer immediately called him to get the details. The next day, to Earl's disgust, Jim began to complain to the press about similar symptoms.

"Don't ask me anything about it," Earl said when reporters quizzed him. "All I know is Jim talked to Wayne, and now he's worried about his rotor cuff." A reporter might have tried to point out that it was rotator, not rotor, but Earl would not have listened. All he cared about was that his best pitcher was complaining about something new.

Despite these complaints, though, Palmer suddenly got into a groove, allowing only three earned runs over the next 67 innings. "I guess Jim's rotor must not be totally torn," said Earl with more than a little sarcasm.

Weaver and Palmer were arguing in the O's' dugout during a game. Since the 6-foot-3 Palmer stood about eight inches taller than his manager, Earl got up on the top step of the dugout and started jumping up and down to make his point.

"Why, Earl," said Palmer, "I've never seen you so tall."

★   ★   ★

Weaver was driving in town one day when a policeman pulled him over for speeding. As the cop looked over his license, he asked if Earl had any physical infirmities.

"Sure I do," he said. "Jim Palmer."

One year the Orioles went on a tour of Japan, playing exhibition games around the country with Japanese professional teams. At one stop, a sumo wrestler visited the O's' clubhouse and, to show how strong he was, lifted Earl up and raised him above his head.

"Drop him!" yelled the Orioles players (good-naturedly, of course). "Drop him!"

The wrestler did not drop him. He set him safely back down.

Baseball can be tough on family life, and it was hard on Weaver, whose first marriage ended in divorce. After he remarried, his second wife said to him, "You spend more time on baseball than you do with my daughter and me. Do you love baseball more than us?"

"Well," Earl replied, "without baseball, we don't eat so good."

Weaver walked away from the game in 1986 after 17 seasons with the Orioles. His teams won six American League East titles, four pennants, and one World Series.

"When *This Week in Baseball* comes on TV, I'll be on the golf course and couldn't care less," he said at the time. "And a year after that, nobody will remember Earl Weaver." Not quite. In 1996, a half-dozen years after Jim Palmer gained entry to the Hall, Weaver won election to Cooperstown.

Turk Wendell

When reliever Steven Wendell (better known as "Turk") was breaking in with the Cubs in the early '90s, he would not catch balls thrown back to him by the umpire behind the plate. He considered them unlucky or something. One time he let an ump's toss hit him in the chest rather than catch it with his glove. Finally, the baffled men in blue gave in to Turk's unusual habit and started rolling the ball out to him.

The umps would not be the last people in the majors who would find Turk's behavior rather peculiar. Before the start of each inning he pitches, Turk faithfully waves to the center fielder, who almost certainly does not wave back. The reason Turk does this is that when he was in high school his best friend played center and they used to wave to each other at the start of innings.

Sometimes when his catcher stands up, Turk will go into a crouch on the mound, just for the heck of it. He has been known to chew licorice at games and brush his teeth between innings. Apparently a hunter in the off-season, he wears a necklace that supposedly contains a tooth of every animal he's killed.

"If they think I'm weird and that gives me an edge," Turk was saying one day, "I'll use it to help my team." They definitely do think Turk is a little weird, they being not only umpires and opposing players but members of his own team. After leaving the Cubs, Turk came over to the Mets, where one of his teammates, Al Leiter (who has a bit of an offbeat reputation himself), described him as being "a couple of cards short of a full deck."

Entering in the late innings of a tight game, Turk got ripped and the Mets lost. Disgusted with himself, he threw his glove into the stands as he was leaving the field, explaining, "It was like if you were dating a girl and not having a good time. You dump her and get a new one."

Turk confided to Leiter that one of the reasons he did it was to see if he could get on ESPN. And sure enough, the glove-tossing made it onto the *SportsCenter* highlights that night.

Wildlife

Casey Stengel broke in with Brooklyn in 1912 and played with the Dodgers for six seasons. As colorful when he was young as he was when he was older, Casey charmed Brooklyn fans with his quirky personality.

By 1918, Stengel had overstayed his welcome in Brooklyn, which sent him to Pittsburgh. When, as a member of the Pirates, he returned to Ebbets Field for the first time after the trade, he heard boos from Dodger loyalists when he appeared on the field. Standing out near the bullpen, Casey saw a sparrow crash against a wall. Stunned from the collision, it lay on the ground. Looking quickly around to see if anyone else had seen what happened, Casey picked the bird up and ran into the Pirates' dugout.

The next inning he came out of the dugout to bat, Brooklyn fans booing him soundly as they had before. Smiling at the reaction of the crowd, Casey doffed his cap—and out flew the sparrow. He had hidden it under his cap, just for this moment; when his cap lifted, the revived sparrow took wing. Amazed by what they saw, the fans stopped booing and started cheeering. Casey Stengel, the magician, was back in town.

At a 1984 game between the Blue Jays and the visiting Yankees, Exhibition Stadium in Toronto was having its usual problems with seagulls. Well, it was a problem for Yankees players, at any rate, as one particularly bothersome gull buzzed the head of third baseman Graig Nettles and swooped past the pitcher's mound before landing on the grass in right center field.

This was in the middle of the fifth, and the Yankees were taking their warm-up tosses. Center fielder Dave Winfield, who was playing catch with Don Baylor in right, decided to scare the gull away by throwing a ball at him. His throw, perhaps more accurate than he expected, bounced once on the synthetic turf and nailed the bird in the neck. "Right away I know he's a goner," said Winfield, who watched the bird fall over instantly. Dead.

After inspecting the bird, Winfield and Baylor summoned a Yankees batboy, who ran onto the field, wrapped the lifeless creature in a towel, and hurriedly exited. As soon as the 36,000-plus fans realized that the bird was dead and Winfield's throw had killed it, loud, rancorous booing filled the stadium. Some fans threw things at Winfield, too.

The Yankees won the game, 3 to 1, and Winfield aided the New York cause with a home run. But while he was doing a postgame interview in the clubhouse—extremely apologetic, Winfield said he never meant to harm the bird and felt awful about it—the Toronto police arrived to take him away. The personable 6-foot-6-inch outfielder had no choice but to squeeze his long legs into the backseat of a squad car and take a ride to the police station.

"I felt like John Dillinger holed up with the hostages," he said, describing the scene when he arrived. The media were swarming the place. Also present was the dead gull. Police apparently needed its body for evidence. Winfield was charged with "unlawfully and willfully" causing injury to the bird, in violation of the criminal code. Bail was set at $500.

Still apologetic, Winfield paid the bill and the charges were dropped. The boo birds were out in force for the next game in Toronto, and for the rest of the season, fans around the league heckled him with gusto, some of them flapping their arms in imitation of a bird.

Although the gull's death upset many people, one of them was not Graig Nettles. "What the hell good is a seagull?" he said, when asked for his reaction to the incident. "I think Winfield should have been given a medal for killing the damn thing."

And Yankees manager Billy Martin offered his own opinion of Winfield's throw: "That was the first time he hit the cutoff man all season."

During a storm in the late eighties, a bald eagle chick fell from its nest in the forest. Some passersby spotted the chick on the ground and picked it up, turning it in to wildlife authorities, who fed the bird and cared for it and eventually returned it to the wild. But other people later spotted this same eagle begging for food in an area frequented by humans. Again the bird entered the care of wildlife officials, who again returned it to the forest. But when it appeared once more in a human area begging for food, a man tried to beat it with a stick. This time, bird rescue people decided the eagle could not live in the wild and must remain in captivity.

The name of this bald eagle, now grown to adulthood, is Challenger, the first bald eagle trained to fly free in public places. Although Challenger had performed at Yankee Stadium for postseason games before 9/11, none of his appearances there was as dramatic as the ones he made during the 2001 World Series. After the playing of the national anthem, Challenger's handlers released him from the blackened area beyond the center-field fence. The bird then flew across the diamond to his chief trainer, Al Cecere, standing on the pitcher's mound. As Cecere stretched out his gloved hand, Challenger spread his wings and landed while people roared their approval.

These appearances, witnessed by a city and nation still grieving from the attacks of September 11, turned the orphan bird into an American celebrity. Performing at major league ballparks and other public spaces around the country, Challenger was in such demand that by the 2003 World Series between the Yankees and Marlins, he could not make it to Yankee Stadium on Sunday night because he was performing earlier in the day at an NFL game in Minneapolis.

Yankees owner George Steinbrenner, however, wanted the bird to be there, and he had the resources to see that his wishes were fulfilled. First he sent his private jet to pick up Challenger, Cecere, and other members of the support team at their bird rescue center in Tennessee. Then they flew to Minneapolis. As soon as the eagle did his thing at the start of the game, the crew climbed into a vehicle waiting outside the Metrodome and drove to the airport, where Steinbrenner's jet took them to Teterboro Airport in New Jersey.

From Teterboro, the New Jersey police provided a motorcycle escort to the New York state line. When the van carrying Challenger crossed the border, the New York police took over, moving rapidly through traffic in order to reach the Bronx before the start of the game.

They made it. Challenger got to Yankee Stadium in time to soar across the diamond.

About the CD

The attached CD was specifically produced as bonus material for *"So Hank Says to Yogi . . ."* It was recorded live at the Chateau Briand in Carle Place, New York, on November 18, 2004. Many thanks to the members of the Winning Beyond Winning organization for their cooperation; to Bob Wolff for assembling and hosting our panel of baseball personalities; to our panel members (listed below); to executive producer Carlo DeVito; and to associate producers Dan DePasquale and Ron Martirano.

Ryne Duren's nine-plus seasons in the majors were highlighted by three all-star appearances (1958, '59, and '61), and a brilliant postseason for the Yankees in 1958, when he went 1–1 with a 1.93 ERA and a save, contributing to New York's title over the Braves. "Blind" Ryne used his "wild thing" reputation to lead the league in saves, also in 1958, with 20.

Bob Feller was regarded as the fastest pitcher of his day, and was voted baseball's greatest living right-handed pitcher in 1969. Giving four seasons to his country during World War II, Feller remains the winningest pitcher in Cleveland Indians history. His induction to the Hall of Fame in 1962 marked the first time a pitcher had been elected on his first ballot since charter member Walter Johnson.

Mudcat Grant's 14-year major-league career reached its pinnacle in 1965, with Minnesota. On their way to the pennant, he led the Twins in victories, winning percentage, and shutouts, and capped off the year with two wins and a three-run homer in the World Series.

Rich Marazzi is a member of the Society for American Baseball Research, a columnist for *Sports Collectors Digest* and *Baseball Digest,* and the author of two baseball books.

Joe Pignatano was the last Brooklyn Dodger to catch at Ebbets Field. A member of Brooklyn's 1959 World Series team, he followed Gil Hodges to the Mets as a coach in 1968.

Ron Swoboda's diving catch in Game 4 and game-winning RBI in Game 5 of the 1969 World Series helped the Miracle Mets win their first title in franchise history.

Frank Torre tied a National League mark in 1957, by scoring six runs in one game. That year he hit two home runs in the World Series to help his Braves beat the Yankees.

Bob Wolff, a baseball Hall of Fame sportscaster, is also a member of the National Sportscasters and Sportswriters Hall of Fame, and the Madison Square Garden Walk of Fame. Wolff is TV's longest-running sportscaster and a former play-caller on NBC's *Game of the Week;* he has been at the mike for three World Series, including the Don Larsen perfect game. He is also the first sportscaster to have done play-by-play for championships in all four major professional sports. Wolff is one of baseball's premier interviewers, and his baseball scrapbook series, aired on the Madison Square Garden network in 2003, won the PowerAde National Award for Best Sports Series of the year. He is currently seen and heard on MSG and Cablevision News 12.